Editor
Eric Migliaccio

Managing Editor
Ina Massler Levin, M.A.

Illustrator
Vicki Frazier

Cover Artist
Barb Lorseyedi

Art Manager
Kevin Barnes

Art Director
CJae Froshay

Imaging
Rosa C. See

Publisher
Mary D. Smith, M.S. Ed.

SEPT
DAILY JOURNAL
WRITING PROMPTS

Author

Maria Elvira Gallardo, M.A.

Teacher Created Resources

Teacher Created Resources, Inc.
6421 Industry Way
Westminster, CA 92683
www.teachercreated.com
ISBN-1-4206-3126-8
©2005 Teacher Created Resources, Inc.
Reprinted, 2006
Made in U.S.A.

Table of Contents

Introduction

More than ever, it is important for students to practice writing on a daily basis. Every classroom teacher knows that the key to getting students excited about writing is introducing interesting topics that are fun to write about. *September Daily Journal Writing Prompts* provides K–2 teachers with an entire month of ready-to-use journal topics, including special holiday and seasonal topics for September. All journal topics are included in a calendar that is easily reproduced for students. A student journal cover allows students to personalize their journal for the month.

Other useful pages that are fun include:

✣ A Blank Calendar (pages 6 and 7)

This can be used to meet your own classroom needs. You may want your students to come up with their own topics for the month, or it may come in handy for homework writing topics.

✣ Word Banks (pages 40–43)

These include commonly used vocabulary words for school, holiday, and seasonal topics. A blank word bank gives students a place to write other words they have learned throughout the month.

✣ September Author Birthdays (page 44)

Celebrate famous authors' birthdays or introduce an author that is new to your students. This page includes the author's birthdays and titles of some of their most popular books.

✣ September Historic Events (page 45)

In the format of a time line, this page is a great reference tool for students. They will love seeing amazing events that happened in September.

✣ September Discoveries & Inventions (page 46)

Kindle students' curiosity about discoveries and inventions with this page. This is perfect to use for your science and social studies classes.

Motivate your students' writing by reproducing the pages in this book and making each student an individual journal. Use all the journal topics included, or pick and choose them as you please. See the Binding Ideas on page 48 for ways to put it all together. Planning a month of writing will never be easier!

Monthly Calendar

S E P T

1 On the first day of school…	**2** No one but me knows…	**3** When it's rainy weather, I…	**4** My favorite animal is…
9 The best time I ever had was…	**10** Something strange that I have seen is…	**11** The best part of school is…	**12** When I first wake up…
17 I have always wanted to…	**18** My favorite activity is…	**19** I wish my parents…	**20** Having a pet is…
25 I feel so happy when...	**26** Homework is…	**27** What I like the most about myself is…	**28** When I'm bored…

Monthly Calendar *(cont.)*

E M B E R

5 On weekends I like to…	**6** I was really embarrassed when…	**7** After school I always…	**8** I always laugh when…
13 Playing games is fun because…	**14** My best friend is…	**15** It makes me tired when…	**16** When I grow up, I want to be…
21 I love reading…	**22** If I had three wishes…	**23** I want to learn all about…	**24** What really drives me crazy is…
29 If only my teacher…	**30** I would love to visit…	**Special Topics** **Labor Day** A good job is important because… **Autumn** My favorite part of autumn…	

Blank Monthly Calendar

S	E	P	T
1	2	3	4
9	10	11	12
17	18	19	20
25	26	27	28

Blank Monthly Calendar *(cont.)*

E M B E R			
5	6	7	8
13	14	15	16
21	22	23	24
29	30	Free Choice Topic	

On the first day of school _____

_____

_____

_____

_____

_____

_____

_____

_____

No one but me knows _____

_____

_____

_____

_____

_____

_____

_____

When it's rainy weather, I _____

_____

_____

_____

_____

_____

_____

_____

_____

My favorite animal is _____

_____

_____

_____

_____

_____

_____

_____

On weekends I like to _____

_____

_____

_____

_____

_____

_____

_____

_____

I was really embarassed when _____

_____

_____

_____

_____

_____

_____

_____

_____

After school I always _____

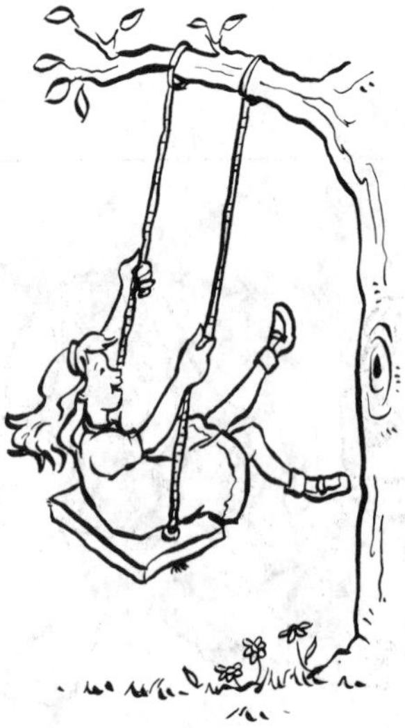

_____

_____

_____

_____

_____

_____

_____

I always laugh when _____

_____

_____

_____

_____

_____

_____

_____

_____

The best time I ever had was _____

_____

_____

_____

_____

_____

_____

_____

Something strange that I have seen is _____

The best part of school is _____

_____

_____

_____

_____

_____

_____

_____

When I first wake up _____

_____

_____

_____

_____

_____

_____

_____

_____

Playing games is fun because _____

_____

_____

_____

_____

_____

_____

_____

_____

My best friend is _____

_____

_____

_____

_____

_____

_____

_____

_____

It makes me tired when _____

_____

_____

_____

_____

_____

_____

_____

When I grow up, I want to be _____

_____

_____

_____

_____

_____

_____

_____

I have always wanted to _____

_____

_____

_____

_____

_____

_____

_____

My favorite activity is _____

_____

_____

_____

_____

_____

_____

_____

_____

I wish my parents _____

_____

_____

_____

_____

_____

_____

_____

_____

Having a pet is _____

_____

_____

_____

_____

_____

_____

_____

_____

I love reading _____

_____

_____

_____

_____

_____

_____

_____

28

If I had three wishes _____

_____

_____

_____

_____

_____

_____

_____

_____

_____

I want to learn all about _____

_____

_____

_____

_____

_____

_____

_____

_____

30

What really drives me crazy is _____

_____

_____

_____

_____

_____

_____

_____

_____

I feel so happy when _____

_____

_____

_____

_____

_____

_____

_____

_____

32

Homework is _____

_____

_____

_____

_____

_____

_____

_____

What I like the most about myself is _____

_____

_____

_____

_____

_____

_____

_____

_____

When I'm bored _____

_____

_____

_____

_____

_____

_____

_____

_____

If only my teacher _____

_____

_____

_____

_____

_____

_____

_____

33 + 22 = _____

_____

I would love to visit _____

_____

_____

_____

_____

_____

_____

_____

A good job is important because _____

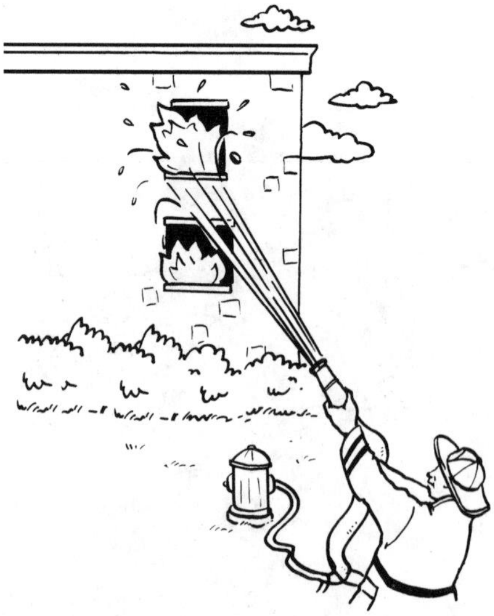

_____

_____

_____

_____

_____

_____

_____

My favorite part of autumn is _____

_____

_____

_____

_____

_____

_____

_____

_____

School Word Bank

activity	desks	map	recess
art	dictionary	markers	report
assembly	flag	math	ruler
award	games	music	science
backpack	glue	office	scissors
board	grades	paper	spelling
books	history	pencils	students
calendar	homework	pens	subject
classroom	learn	playground	teacher
computer	library	principal	test
crayons	lunch	reading	write

Holiday Word Bank

September Holidays

American Indian Day

Labor Day

Rosh Hashanah (Jewish New Year, Day of Remembrance)

Yom Kippur (Jewish Day of Atonement)

Grandparents' Day

Mexican Independence Day

career	government	relatives
caring	grandma	religious
celebrate	grandpa	revolution
challah	holy	shofar
culture	honor	special
customs	job	symbols
education	kin	synagogue
family	loving	traditions
festival	parade	tribes
forgiveness	prayers	workers

Seasonal Word Bank

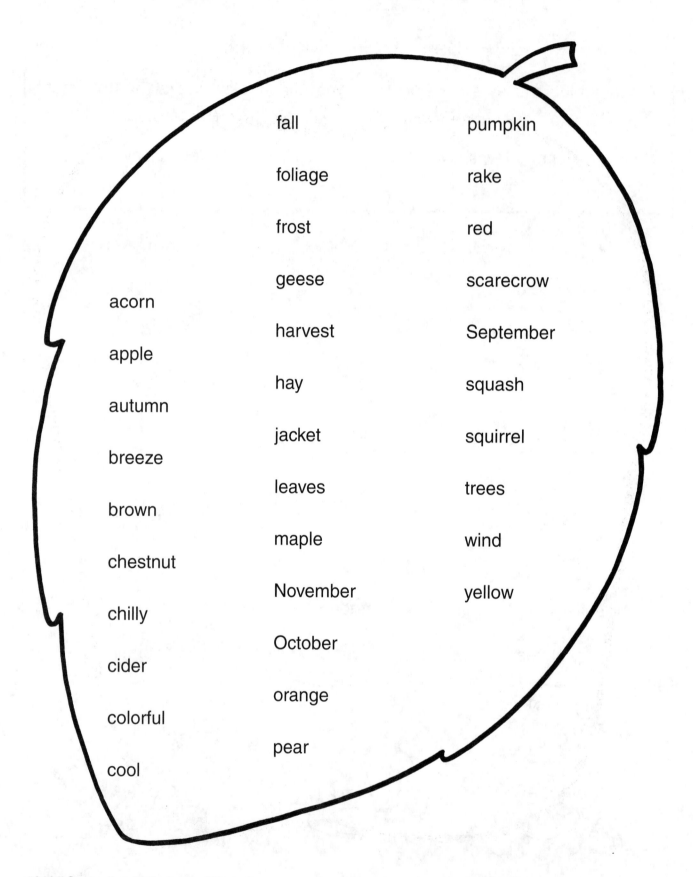

acorn

apple

autumn

breeze

brown

chestnut

chilly

cider

colorful

cool

fall

foliage

frost

geese

harvest

hay

jacket

leaves

maple

November

October

orange

pear

pumpkin

rake

red

scarecrow

September

squash

squirrel

trees

wind

yellow

My Word Bank

September Author Birthdays

3

Aliki
(b. 1929)

A Medieval Feast
(1983, Ty Crowell Co.)
Feelings
(1984, Harper Collins)

8

Jon Scieszka
(b. 1954)

The Stinky Cheese Man (1992, Viking)
The True Story of the Three Little Pigs!
(1996, Puffin)

13

Roald Dahl
(1916–1990)

James and the Giant Peach (1961, Knopf)
Charlie and the Chocolate Factory (1964, Knopf)

15

Tomie DePaola
(b. 1934)

26 Fairmont Avenue
(1999, Putnam)
Here We All Are
(2000, Putnam)

16

H.A. Rey
(1898–1977)

Curious George
(1941, Houghton Mifflin)
Curious George Gets a Medal
(1957, Houghton Mifflin)

18

Joanne Ryder
(b. 1946)

The Snail's Spell
(1998, Puffins)
Earthdance
(1999, Henry Holt)
Come Along, Kitten
(2003, Simon & Schuster)

21

Taro Yashima
(b. 1908)

Crow Boy
(1955, Viking Press)
Momo's Kitten
(1961, Viking Press)

22

Olivier Dunrea
(b. 1953)

Bear Noel
(2000, Farrar Straus & Giroux)
It's Snowing!
(2002, Farrar Straus & Giroux)

25

Shel Silverstein
(1930–1999)

The Giving Tree
(1964, Harper & Row)
Where the Sidewalk Ends
(1974, Harper & Row)
A Light in the Attic
(1981, Harper & Row)

27

Bernard Waber
(b. 1924)

Lyle, Lyle, Crocodile
(1973, Walter Lorraine Books)
Loveable Lyle (1977, Walter Lorraine Books)

29

Marissa Moss
(b. 1959)

Amelia's Notebook
(1995, Ten Speed Press)
Amelia Writes Again
(1999, Pleasant Company)

29

Stan Berenstain
(b. 1924)

The Berenstain Bears' New Baby
(1974, Random House)
The Berenstain Bears Go to School (1978, Random House)

September   Historic   Events

September 4, 1781
The city of Los Angeles was founded in southwest California.

September 5, 1882
The first labor day parade was held in New York City.

September 7, 1909
The first junior high school was opened in Columbus, Ohio.

September 9, 1850
California became the 31st state of the United States.

September 12, 1959
Luna 2, the first spacecraft to land on the moon, was launched by the USSR.

September 16, 1620
The *Mayflower* left Plymouth, England and landed in what is now Massachusetts two months later.

September 17, 1787
The Constitution was approved and signed in Pennsylvania.

September 19, 1928
Walt Disney debuted Mickey Mouse in a cartoon called *Steamboat Willie.*

September 20, 1519
Magellan led the first expedition to travel completely around the globe.

September 22, 1862
Abraham Lincoln freed the slaves in the Emancipation Proclamation.

September 24, 1957
For the first time, African-American and white students attended the same school in Little Rock, Arkansas.

September Discoveries & Inventions

4
The first electric lighting by Thomas Edison in 1882. Four hundred electric lights lit up offices in lower Manhattan, New York.

Kodak camera patented by George Eastman in 1888. He further invented photographic film and paper that enable people to take photographs.

12 **Prehistoric paintings** were discovered in 1940 by five boys playing in a cave in southwestern France.

18 **Crayola Crayons** were created for kids in 1903 by Edwin Binney and C. Harold Smith in Pennsylvania.

21
Bubble gum was invented in 1928 by Walter Diemer. He called his invention "Dubble Bubble."

Velcro was created in 1955 by George de Mestral in Switzerland.

22 **It's the ice-cream cone's birthday**. It was invented in 1903 by Italo Marchiony.

21
The planet Neptune was seen for the first time by German astronomers J.C. Galle and H.d' Arrest in 1846.

The Pacific Ocean was discovered in 1513 by Vasco Nunez de Balboa, a Spanish conquistador.

25 **The zipper gets its name** by B.F. Goodrich in 1923. It was previously called the "separable fastener" and "clasp locker."

28 **Discovery of California** in 1542 by Portuguese navigator Juan Rodriguez Cabrillo, who reached San Diego Bay.

30 **The patent for the stapler** was granted to Samuel Slocum in 1841. He called it a machine "for sticking pins into paper."

September

Journal

by

_____

Binding Ideas

Students will be so delighted when they see a month of their writing come together with one of the following binding ideas. You may choose to bind their journals at the beginning or end of the month, once they have already filled all of the journal topic pages. When ready to bind students' journals, have them color in their journal cover on page 47. It may be a good idea to reproduce the journal covers on hard stock paper in order to better protect the pages in the journal. Use the same hard stock paper for the back cover.

Simple Book Binding

1. Put all pages in order and staple together along the left margin.

2. Cut book-binding tape to the exact length of the book.

3. Run the center line of tape along the left side of the book and fold to cover the front left margin and the back right margin. Your book is complete!

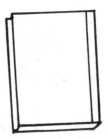

Yarn-Sewn Binding

1. Put all pages in order and hole-punch the left margin.

2. Stitch the pages together with thick yarn or ribbon.

BENJAMIN BALDWIN
An Autobiography in Design

*This book is dedicated to many who have touched my life
with the magic of friendship and love.*

BENJAMIN BALDWIN
An Autobiography in Design

Foreword by Michael Rubin

W.W. Norton & Company

New York London

A NORTON PROFESSIONAL BOOK

Printed in Singapore

First Edition

Edited by Cynthia Newman Bohn
Designed by Shirley Weese Young and Arthur Beckenstein
Typeset in Palatino by Deborah Zeidenberg
Printed and bound in Singapore by Tien Wah Press

Library of Congress Cataloging-in-Publication Data

Baldwin, Benjamin, 1913–1993.
    Benjamin Baldwin: an autobiography in design / introduction by Michael Rubin.
        p.   cm.
    Includes bibliographical references.
    ISBN 0-393-70198-0
    1. Baldwin, Benjamin, 1913–1993. 2. Interior decorators—United States—Biography. I. Title.
NK2004.3.B33A2   1995
729'.092—dc20   94-23892
                                                                                    CIP

ISBN 0-393-70198-0

W.W. Norton & Company, Inc., 500 Fifth Avenue, New York, NY 10110
W.W. Norton & Company, Ltd., 10 Coptic Street, London WC1A 1PU

0 9 8 7 6 5 4 3 2 1

Contents

Foreword

The poet Yeats once said that the English mind is rich, meditative, and deliberate. Bernard Jones, the music critic, made a similar observation in characterizing certain contemporary composers as empirical and contemplative, rather than theoretical and dramatic. Ben Baldwin's work seems to embody the spirit of this sentiment. Although trained as an architect, he was not limited by purely formal concerns. In his work issues of space and structure are combined with equal concern for texture and color. Whether designing a chair, a house, or a garden, Ben let the act of designing inform the finished work in a way that makes the result seem inevitable. I have never known anyone with his dedication to finding the appropriate, balanced, and emotionally calming solution to design problems. Perhaps this is what Louis Kahn meant when he characterized Ben as *the* classic interior designer.

Ben liked simple things. Of course, he was an immensely sophisticated man, yet he never let any of that get in the way of appreciating basics. A great example of this is that Ben once told me he liked flowers, not flower arrangements. This is not to say there are no situations or occasions when such conspicuous arrangements would not be appropriate. Ben was simply wary of enterprises that are precious or pretentious.

In a time when the design world is preoccupied with concerns of image and intellectual gamesmanship, it is refreshing to realize that Ben went his own way, bringing out the character of whatever he was working with, be it furniture, paintings, or plants, without himself getting in the way. The effects are subtle. Ben's sensitivity to works of art, for example, considered not only the work itself but how it would look with everything else in the spatial composition.

Like all truly creative people, Ben defied labeling. His appreciation of a Japanese sense of space has, at times, given him the tag of minimalist, although one of his most successful chair designs is the reworking of a Baroque precedent. His Huntting Lane house and garden used an architectural vocabulary that is no doubt modernist while his Palma Terrace project exploited arched trellises for white roses in a way that recalls traditional English gardens. Because labels are at best convenient generalizations, they cannot define the subtleties and complexities of this meditative man. This is why I am so happy that Ben wrote his autobiography.

Michael Rubin, Architect

The Beginnings

The Beginnings

Left My great-grandfather's house on Madison Avenue, Montgomery, Alabama. *Above* My mother and I, upon the occasion of my christening, 1913.

It consoles me to know that the great Armory Show was installed in New York at the same time I was born in the bosom of the Confederacy. The year was 1913, the place a house right across the street from the Alabama Capitol in Montgomery—the first capital of the Confederacy. The capitol still stands on its bump of a hill with its worn brass star where Jeff Davis stood. Dexter Avenue still rolls down straight as an Indian arrow to Court Square and the big fountain by Frederick Macmonnies (who designed the big fountain at the 1893 Columbian Exposition in Chicago) with its tiers of cherubs and the Southern lady on top sprinkling her waters. The Confederate flag still flies.

My long series of love affairs with houses began with the big old house on Madison Avenue where my great-grandfather had lived and after him my grandfather. We moved there after my grandparents had moved to a house nearby. Our new home was only a few blocks away from my birthplace, but it was on a much grander scale and a child's paradise. In those days Madison Avenue was a majestic street, very wide, with many gracious houses and huge magnolia trees shading the sidewalks. Our two-story house, made of brick that had been stuccoed over, was on a large lot.

I had several favorite places to play. One was the cool back porch, which had dark green moveable shutters all across the outside wall and a wooden swing hung on chains. Under this porch was the entrance to the basement, a world of true make-believe, with brick floors and brick columns topped by arches. There were many rooms down there in the dim light, all with closed doors and each packed with treasures—an old leather sidesaddle, a pair of short marble columns with metal busts in dark colors, a billy-goat wagon made of wood slats with a front and back seat.

At one end of the back porch was the little house where our nurse lived. I can't imagine what we did to deserve having Ida Adams in our lives, but I believe that whatever goodness there may be in me is surely her doing. A person of such beauty and patience and love, she appeared every morning in her clean blue-grey dress with its starched white collar pinned at the bosom with a big silver pin, an Indian head with a full feather headdress. She herself was part Indian. She'd get us dressed, and off we'd go for our early morning walk.

When the weather was not good enough to be outside, we were

allowed to play in the ballroom, a separate one-story structure attached to the house on the garden side. The windows of this big square room looked out into the garden over a bed of speckled yellow cannas and four o'clocks. I remember once seeing the room used for its intended purpose when my parents entertained at a gala dinner, and we children were allowed to sit near the top of the stairs and watch the guests arriving. The square oak table my great-grandfather had had made for the room was opened up with all its leaves and in its center was a real fountain with tiny jets of water. This was surrounded by silver candlesticks in which pale candles were shaded by filigreed silver shades lined with pink silk. The room was filled with big bunches of pastel sweet peas which smelled delicious.

I have often been asked how it is that certain people become designers and spend their lives working with places in which other people will live and things other people will use—with houses, furniture, and gardens. At this early stage there was little to indicate that I would devote my life to design rather than becoming a farmer, a long-distance telephone operator, or a merchant seaman. Perhaps there were indications of my future in the fact that I always liked to make things with my hands—puppets, sand castles, peepshows inside holes in the ground lined with soft green moss and covered over with broken pieces of glass. At a young age I put on theatrical productions, doing the sets, costumes, and lighting, as well as acting and performing special dance numbers.

My grandfather—my father's father—had a lot to do with shaping my future. He had retired from his practice of medicine when he was about thirty-eight, after which he and my grandmother spent a lot of time traveling all over the world. My favorite picture of them as tourists was taken in front of the Sphinx; both of them are elegantly dressed and sitting on camels, my grandmother in a voluminous black dress, a huge hat with plumes, and long black gloves that entirely covered her arms. Their enthusiasm for travel was passed on to me, but with less luggage involved. I started going on trips with them when I was quite young—to the Grove Park Inn outside Asheville, North Carolina, to Warm Springs, Georgia, and later by train to Savannah and on to New York by boat. We went to Chalfont-Haddon Hall (with its after-dinner string quartets) in Atlantic City and to Chicago, where we took a boat around the Great Lakes and up the St. Lawrence Seaway to Quebec.

My second love affair was with Hazel Hedge—not a lady, but a house. Actually Hazel Hedge *was* Jean Read—my favorite cousin on the Baldwin side. Without her it was simply a big wooden ark of a place on the outskirts of Montgomery that was being actively eaten up by termites and dry rot. In winter the heat was unpredictable and the pipes froze. There were always repairs under way—on the big rambling roof, the wood on the arbors, the floorboards in the porches. In summer it breathed in the warm air from the shaded lawns that encircled it, pulled through the rooms by a big attic fan. Architecturally it was a house no one would have looked at twice. But with Jean there it became an ever-changing set for make-believe and magic. Jean looked and sounded like a character out of an English play. Tall and thin as a beanpole, she ate almost nothing and never slept, preferring to read most of the night. She was full of delightful conversation and wonderful stories made even more fascinating by bits of inaccurate information, and she gave herself with complete enthusiasm to living life and to giving people pleasure. She worked in her garden like a field hand, did sets for the little theatre with furniture from her own house, decorated weddings with so many candles that everything caught fire in the middle of the ceremony. She arranged costume parties on the lawn and beautiful picnics in the country by sandy creeks where we could wade in the cool water.

The property at Hazel Hedge was surrounded by a dense hedge of yucca, bamboo, and pink roses. In the front yard was a small pool near an enormous elm whose branches covered most of the yard like a giant umbrella. In the spring masses of daffodils and rain lilies bloomed in the grass around the tree. The elm was a personage—a spirit—and when it finally died of old age it was like a death in the family. On one side of the house was a screened porch with garlands of pomegranates all around its edges. On the porch were cupboards painted by Jean, iron stands ringed with candles, and gauze Chinese lanterns hanging from the ceiling. Lambo, a black poodle, had pushed holes in the screens going in and out to the garden, which surrounded the porch on two sides. A long arbor covered with wisteria and roses led to a fountain. Mounds of pink azaleas, lilies, and big rice-paper plants lined the hedges, beyond which were beds of roses and a high garden wall with yellow *banksia* roses cascading over it and climbing up into the tall cedar trees. Near the porch was a well with a bucket and a painted della Robbia plaque; a column of Confederate jasmine twined up to the eaves and mixed its fragrance with that of a huge clump of white ginger lilies.

In good weather, we usually had our meals on the screened porch, but on special occasions they were served in the adjoining dining room with its big fireplace. There a dining table and Queen Anne chairs sat on a worn Oriental rug at the end of which was a big carved Spanish chest. The gold and white china in the tall highboy was reflected in the ceiling-high pier mirror opposite.

The drawing room of the house, which gave the place its English country feeling, was full of sunshine, filtered through gold gauze in winter and cooled by green gauze in summer. On both sides of the fireplace books spilled out of the shelves onto tables and chairs. The furnishings here—a big overstuffed sofa, tufted in worn brown velvet, a cane chaise and chairs, a long carved wooden bench, a small Steinway grand, and tables full of flowers—were all casual and comfortable. In the springtime huge branches of cut pear blossoms touched the ceiling and long sprays of yellow roses in amber Venini vases and paper-white narcissus in green pottery bowls stood next to small vases of pink camellias. In summer the room was like an enchanted place under the sea. The gold gauze curtains were changed to green and the vases were filled with tropical-looking rice-paper leaves. All the furniture was slipcovered in green and white and the rugs were put away in the cedar closets. During the Christmas season, when Jean gathered her many friends of all ages to sing carols and drink her lethal punch, the room danced with golden candlelight and with shadows from the fire of oak logs. The house was happy and full of laughter.

I went to Hazel Hedge whenever I needed to reinforce my feeling that life should be full of wonder and beauty. Sometimes I stayed overnight in the big pink guest room with its four-poster bed sitting high off the floor. We made puppets or played charades and murder with all the lights turned off. My favorite times were those alone with Jean in the yellow sitting room downstairs, with a coal fire in the grate and pots of white Roman hyacinths in the big bay window facing the garden. I always went straight to Jean if I were planning a trip to Europe, and she shared with me her endless store of information. She was the first person to tell me about the enchanted gardens of the Villa Lante near Rome.

Jean is buried now in the old cemetery under ancient magnolias where star of Bethlehem pushes up through the grass in the spring. But she and Hazel Hedge taught me the greatest lesson—that living and working are part of the same thing and must be done with joy and

total awareness, that a house is a shelter in a garden and that living there is what makes it beautiful.

And then there was Kintray—the enchanted castle of my childhood—built by my grandfather near the little village of Verbena, Alabama, about thirty miles north of Montgomery. In the summer it was much cooler there than in Montgomery, and during an epidemic of yellow fever in the 1870s a number of prominent men had moved their families out to this area. My great-grandfather built a house called Roll-em-High right in the village, and some time later my grandfather bought a hundred and fifty acres of wooded land nearby, on the banks of Chestnut Creek, and built Kintray, which was used only in the summer.

My grandparents would occasionally invite a group of us children to come to Kintray for a house party. We traveled by train—a very slow local which stopped at every little town on the way and took an hour and a half to go the thirty miles. Meeting the afternoon train was a special event in Verbena. Most people waited for the mail to be sorted and put in pigeonholes in the tiny post office next to the deserted old hotel, which had been built during the short time Verbena flourished as a resort. Grandfather met us in the trap, a chrome yellow buggy with seats facing front and back and a fringed top. The sleek black horse was named Killarney and wore long strings of beads which my grandparents had bought in the Holy Land on one of their trips. Our route went over the noisy red bridge across Chestnut Creek to the entrance to Kintray, where we stopped to pull the wooden handle that opened the gate. The long curving road went past a rustic gazebo perched on the side of the hill overlooking the old dam across Chestnut Creek. Then we could see the house at the top of the hill.

A huge porch stretched across the entire front of the house. On it was a varied collection of rocking chairs with and without arms, hammocks made of woven wire, a big black wicker reclining chair, and an even larger plantation chair with a footrest which could be swung across between the wide arms. A square open terrace, shaded by the limbs of a huge oak tree, extended out over the steep hillside and below it ran Chestnut Creek. The stone walls of the terrace were covered with English ivy, while the stone flower boxes built up around its three sides were planted with lemon verbena, balsam, stokesia, and petunias. Supper was usually wheeled out to this terrace on carts from the kitchen at the back of the house.

As it began to get dark, hundreds of fireflies would appear in the woods that led down to the creek, and if there was a moon the terrace would be covered with shadow patterns from the great oak tree. Its twisted branches were covered with tree ferns, which turned a fresh bright green whenever it rained. There was an endless din of katydids and locusts which had their homes in the tree. No planes disturbed the night silence. There was only the sound of the creek going over the rocks and the songs of the night creatures. Occasionally a train would rumble past in the distance.

Behind the porch was a large central hallway; it had a fireplace almost high enough to stand in, with big black andirons bought in London. Opposite the fireplace was a long seat recessed into the wall with bookshelves above. The seat had cushions and was a favorite place to stretch out after meals. It was lovely on chilly, rainy days to lie here with a fire in the fireplace. We burned large oak logs which were cut on the place and had pine cones to throw into the fire. The hearth and the sides of the big fireplace were faced with deep red rectangular tiles, and on the panel directly above it was carved in wood something my grandmother had written:

In Kintray and with Kith let's find
Good cheer for body, soul and mind.

The floor of the hall was covered with heavy Chinese matting which my grandparents had bought on their travels. Much heavier and more yellow than the thin Japanese matting we see now, it smelled deliciously of fresh straw when we stretched out on the floor after lunch.

Off the right side of the front hall was a large square bedroom used by my grandparents and later by my parents. Like all of the rooms in the front part of the house, it had a very high ceiling. There was a corner fireplace, which backed up to the big fireplace in the central hall, and four tall windows. All the windows were designed so that the lower sash pushed up part way into the ceiling. When the window was open you could look out without having any part of it interfere with your vision. On all of the windows in the front part of the house there were outside shutters painted black-green, which came down to the floor. On the wall opposite the door was a very large four-poster bed with a canopy supported on solid mahogany posts. Across the hall were two more large square bedrooms with a bath between.

From the back of the front hall, one entered the Link, so-called

Left Kintray, view of the front from the hillside approach. *Below* The front porch at Kintray, circa 1915.

Kintray from the side garden; in the center is the Link.

because it joined the front part of the house, which my grandfather had built, with the older part in the back. The Link was a large room of about twenty-four by sixty feet. It ran the full width of the house and had windows across the two ends. These began about three feet off the floor and went all the way to the high ceiling. The walls were tongue-and-groove pine used vertically up to a chair rail and then horizontally above this. The ceiling was made of the same wood.

As you came into the Link from the front hall, at the right was a large dining table (the oak table my great-grandfather had had made for his house in Montgomery) surrounded by high-backed upholstered chairs. Above the table was a very unusual fan with a vertical supporting rod that went through the table and down through the floor, connecting to a water wheel underneath the house. All of my grandmother's white damask tablecloths had to be cut in half and fitted around the rod that supported the fan, which revolved very slowly, about five or six feet above the table.

When my grandparents lived at Kintray, the Link was a sort of catch-place for the mementos they brought back from traveling. There was a long oak table covered with all sorts of souvenirs fascinating to children—shoes from China, Japan, and Holland; pressed tea from India stamped with fancy designs; a wooden wedding bowl from Norway with curved horses' necks for handles; a small Japanese pagoda in lacquered wood; and wooden nutcrackers carved in the shape of rabbit and bear heads. Opposite the dining table, in the sitting area of the Link, there was a large roll-top desk along with an assortment of armchairs. A big rack of antlers rested on a felt-covered table in the center of the room; it held a collection of tennis racquets in canvas cases. On the walls were stuffed and mounted fish and the heads of several goats an uncle of ours had shot when he was living in Alaska. Also in the center of the room was a large square box used for storing the paper lanterns my grandparents had gotten in Japan. We used them occasionally when we had parties out on the terrace. This box had an upholstered cushion on it so it was a favorite place for children to stretch out between projects.

Behind the Link there were smaller rooms with lower ceilings. On the right side of the central hall was a room that was always called "the boys' room," a square bedroom with a window into the Link and two windows onto the outside, with a fireplace between them. Behind this room was a dressing room with cabinets for clothes and a bathroom with a very long bathtub on claw feet and a white marble lavatory.

At about age fifteen, portrait by
Madeline Sharrer.

Across the hall was a square sitting room called "the Blue Room" because of the carpet on the floor. When my grandparents had the house this room was used mostly in the fall or late summer, when they made only rare visits to Kintray. They used to sit back there because it was easy to warm the room with an open fire on chilly nights. When I was a child, we used the room for card games, playing hearts and slapjack at the big round mahogany table. Behind the Blue Room was a small dining room also used in the fall when the weather was cool. When our mother and father and all of us lived there, we ate here most of the time, dining in the Link only on special occasions. Behind the little dining room was a pantry, then the kitchen and more pantries behind that.

Across a small court paved in brick was the servants' house, which had two bedrooms, a bathroom, and a porch. Dilsey, the cook, lived on one side and Sullivan, the butler-driver-handyman, on the other. My grandfather had raised Sullivan at Kintray and in Montgomery. He became part of the household when he was still in his teens and worked for my grandparents until my grandfather died. He was one of the great characters of the world and used to delight all of us children by playing games with us, taking us on possum hunts in the fall, or just telling us stories. Standing on the front terrace, he could throw a rock and hit a knot on a tree all the way on the other side of Chestnut Creek—a real dead-eye shot. He was always in wonderful spirits, always entertaining, and full of philosophical humor.

A little bit further down in the woods was another wooden house where Mose Anderson and his wife Bea lived. Mose ran the farm, which was a separate piece of property a few miles away from Kintray. Mose raised mostly cotton at the farm, which he got to in his wagon pulled by two hefty mules, and did odd jobs at Kintray, cutting the grass, running the pump, and taking care of the vegetable garden. His wife Bea and her sister Irene did all of the laundry.

Also in the woods was a building made of logs that housed a bowling alley. A small porch in front led into an anteroom where the scoreboard was kept, then to the alley itself, which was fairly high off the ground by the time you got to the end with the pins. The bowling alley was lighted at night by very large brass lanterns which burned kerosene. These had glass chimneys and wide metal shades which kept the big brown and yellow moths away. The bowling alley was the site of wonderful tournaments in the summer between visitors and home teams. The home teams usually won because we knew that the floor had a definite tilt to one side and you had to take this into consideration when throwing the ball. Years later, when I had the place, a windstorm took down several hundred pine trees and cut a path through the woods, flattening the alley and scattering the balls and pins.

Verbena, the nearest village to Kintray, had nothing to offer in the way of entertainment, so we had to provide all our own amusement. The bowling alley was used a great deal, and we had a rather dilapidated tennis court where we had almost daily matches. The court had a lot of tree roots and rocks and was a far from perfect surface, but its limitations did not lessen our enthusiasm. We had tournaments that went on for days whenever we had house guests in the summer.

When I was about twelve, we were all taken out of school in Montgomery, and our family spent a year or so living at Kintray, during which we attended public school in Verbena. I will never forget the delight of waking up in my white room very early in the morning on cold winter days and seeing the bright orange reflections from the fire Mose had made while we were still asleep. He would come in about five-thirty and make fires in all the rooms so that by the time we got up the rooms were warm. There was no central heating, but the fireplaces, plus a pot-bellied stove in the Link, did a good job of keeping us warm.

In 1927 we moved back to Montgomery, and the following year, when I was fifteen years old, I was sent away to Lawrenceville, a prep school in New Jersey. My grandfather had decided that I should go to Princeton and study architecture since this seemed to be the most likely thing someone with "artistic" inclinations could do as a practical career. A whole new life started for me at Lawrenceville. For the first time I was really on my own, and I enjoyed this freedom and independence enormously. The campus was very beautiful, and the countryside around the town, with its rolling hills and green fields, was not too unlike Alabama. I loved taking walks along the small country roads outside the village. I had a room by myself on the second floor of Cleve House, with windows looking out over the campus through the thick ivy that grew on the walls of the brick building. My three years at the school were very active ones. I took five courses every year, so my schedule was busy, but I found time to play the lead in the Periwig Club's annual play and to write stories for the school's literary magazine. I also belonged to the Pipe and Quill Club—a literary

group that met once a month in the drawing room of the headmaster's house—played tennis, and ran cross country.

In the summer of my second year at Lawrenceville, I went to Europe for the first time. My grandfather had decided it was time for me to start traveling so he organized the trip. My oldest sister, my maternal grandmother, and a girl cousin went with me as well as a woman doctor who was vaguely related to us. She knew her way around Europe and acted as guide and chaperone. We sailed on the old liner Statendam, with a lot of students, and made the grand tour of the usual places. For the first time in my life I was exposed to the architecture I had seen only in books and saw real paintings in museums. I was especially excited by the contemporary paintings we saw in exhibitions in Germany. The entire trip was very much an eye-opener for me.

In the spring of 1931 I graduated from Lawrenceville and the following fall was accepted to the school of architecture at Princeton, where I spent the following four years. At that time, Jean Labatut was head critic and Shirley Morgan was director of the school. Jim Davis was teaching freehand drawing and painting and making his experimental movies of motion and light reflections—a field in which he was an important pioneer.

I had a stiff schedule of work, but I managed some extracurricular activity. I wrote theatre and movie reviews for the *Daily Princetonian,* which meant that I not only had a pass to the local movies but also got to spend a lot of weekends in New York seeing plays. The Waldorf and a few other hotels that advertised in the *Princetonian* allowed me to stay free of charge, and I would attend three or four plays during the weekend. These stays in New York gave me a chance to go to galleries, museums, and the ballet as well, all of which was great fun.

There were also exciting things to do at Princeton. Plays often tried out at the McCarter Theatre before opening in New York, and there were often dance recitals. Martha Graham came with her troupe, as did Harold Kreutzberg, Mary Wigman, and Uday Shankar—all the early innovators in dance. There were also wonderful concerts. In addition, the English Department sponsored a lecture series. Among the many fascinating speakers were T. S. Eliot (who came twice), Gertrude Stein and Alice B. Toklas, and Le Corbusier, who lectured in French and put up around the entire room a roll of tracing paper on which he made beautiful drawings in colored chalks to illustrate his talk. So I learned as much from the activities going on outside the school of ar-

chitecture as in the school itself, and for the first time in my life became involved in what was going on in the world of the arts.

When I was there Princeton was involved in the Beaux-Arts system, as were most of the schools of architecture at that time, including Yale, Harvard, and Columbia. Students from all the schools did projects developed by the École des Beaux-Arts in Paris, which were then submitted to a jury of architects and designers in New York. Outside critics who were practicing architects came now and then and looked at what we were doing. The one I remember most was George Howe, who had done the Philadelphia Savings Fund (PSF) bank and office tower in Philadelphia with William Lescaze. He invited us all to come to Philadelphia to see the bank as well as a townhouse he had done for the Speizer family. This was the first time I had seen a collection of modern art in a private house. At the time there were very few modern buildings in this country other than Frank Lloyd Wright's early buildings and those of Louis Sullivan in Chicago.

My other extracurricular activity at Princeton was doing sets for the Theatre Intime, a campus group which put on plays with students as actors. Since the university was not coed at the time, they recruited girls from the village or the local school for the female parts. Theatre design as well as painting had always interested me, and I was not sure at this point whether I wanted to go into one of these fields instead of architecture. Thus, when I graduated in 1935 with an A.B. degree in architecture, I decided I would take a year off and study painting to try to decide whether I wanted to become a painter or to continue with my architectural studies. I had a friend at this time named Wilfrid Zogbaum, who was studying with Hans Hofmann, so I talked to him about my dilemma and decided I would go to New York and study at the Hofmann school.

In 1936 Hofmann had been in this country just a short time and was teaching in his own school, located on the top floor of a building on Fifty-seventh Street and Lexington Avenue. I found a small room near the school in the east Sixties—a fifth-floor walk-up which shared a bath with several other rooms. Here I settled down for the winter to study painting. Some of my fellow students became lifelong friends: Ray Kaiser, who afterwards married Charles Eames; Lee Krasner, who later married Jackson Pollock; Mercedes Carles, who later became Mrs. Herbert Matter; and Helen Donnelley from Chicago. Helen had been partly responsible for bringing Hofmann to this country, and she helped support him for a while, until he could get the school

Below, clockwise from top left Painting done while studying with Hofmann. Watercolor (me in Brittany) by Honoré Sharrer. Charcoal figure drawing done at Hofmann school. Portrait of me (by Peter Teigen) done while I was at Princeton. Portrait (me in Province-town) by Mercedes Carles.

under way. Wilf Zogbaum helped run the school and acted as monitor.

This was one of the most important years of my life. Fifty-seventh Street in the mid-1930s was an exciting place to be, and Hofmann was an extraordinary man as well as a great teacher. I learned so much from him both in the classroom and on our many visits to the art galleries located within a few blocks of the school.

In the summer of 1936, I decided to go to Provincetown and continue studying with Hofmann there. He took a house and studio on the hill above the town; a number of us lived there with him and attended classes. Known as the old Hawthorne place, the house was located right on the edge of the dunes where masses of blueberries grew in the sand. We often walked across the dunes to the beach—one of the most beautiful places I have ever seen. Hofmann was taking care of a Pekinese named Chung, which belonged to Wilf Zogbaum's mother, and in the late afternoon the three of us would often walk down through the village to the waterfront and out to the end of the long pier off the main street. I remember with delight the long conversations that ensued.

I think Hofmann was at his best when he was criticizing students' work. He would spend a morning arranging a dozen still lifes, each with its own background of colored fabrics, or carefully posing nude models, then come into the studio when we were drawing or painting these set-ups. After looking at what we were doing, he would take a razor blade and slice the paper into several pieces, then stick it all back together with thumbtacks in an entirely different arrangement. Invariably the result had much more spatial feeling than the original. From this training I learned more about space than I had ever learned from anybody else, even in relation to design and architecture. I came to understand the way colors interact and work together or against one another, the way planes pull in space against one another. This has been very important to me in my work since that time and has enriched my understanding of painting, sculpture, architecture, and landscape design.

By the time the summer school ended, I had decided I would go back to Princeton and complete my graduate work. In 1937 I was awarded the Stuyvesant Prize, given by the Princeton school of architecture to the student most qualified to attend the American School of Fine Arts in Fontainebleau, France. Jean Labutut (who was still head of the school) was going to be at Fontainebleau that summer as a critic, and this provided me with a chance to work with him on the

Peristyle connecting the library
and the museum at the Cranbrook
Academy of Art; in the foreground
is Carl Milles's Triton pool.

designs he was doing for fountains and fireworks for the upcoming 1939 New York World's Fair.

I spent the entire summer in Fontainebleau, but because I didn't especially like the situation in the architectural school, I decided to study sculpture under M. Gélin, who was then head of the sculpture school, rather than architecture. I made some good friends in the music school and spent most of my free time with them. We took weekend trips, visiting Mont-Saint-Michel and other interesting places not too far away. Being so close to Paris, I spent a lot of time there, partly with Labatut, making a lot of movies, especially at night along the Seine, where the fountains and fireworks for the 1937 World's Fair were concentrated.

The Paris Fair was a very exciting experience. The center of the city around the Eiffel Tower was aglow with reflected light. Particularly impressive was the Spanish Pavilion, designed by Luis Sert, for which Picasso had created his mural *Guernica*. The same pavilion had a mercury fountain made by Alexander Calder, the parts of which moved as flowing mercury weighed them down. The most beautiful pavilion, designed by Le Corbusier, was made entirely of multi-colored canvas supported on cables. The space inside was extraordinary with ramps moving through it, connecting the various levels on which were displays and drawings pertaining to urbanism and city planning. The color was planned by Fernand Léger and was so beautiful in itself that the actual exhibits seemed unnecessary. The building was closed by the city because they believed that the materials used made it unsafe. But I did manage to get in, thanks to Jean Labatut, and I will never forget the quality of the light as it shone through the colored canvas.

At the end of the summer, I took a bus trip alone through the château country and ended up in the south of France at Hyères. From there I took a small boat to a very small island called Porquerolles, a few miles out in the Mediterranean. I spent about ten happy days there, mostly swimming and sunbathing or walking around the perimeter of the island in the hot sun.

During my last year at Princeton, I decided I would do my thesis on city planning and took as my project an area in my home town of Montgomery. I replanned a black area centered around State Normal College, a teachers' college for blacks, including a park that, because of segregation, had always been for whites only.

In the spring of 1938 I graduated from Princeton, receiving an M.F.A. degree with honors in architecture, and was awarded a scholarship to the Cranbrook Academy of Art in Bloomfield Hills, Michigan. The scholarship would support my work in city planning under Eliel Saarinen, who was then head of the school of design at Cranbrook. Seven architectural students, each one from a different college, had been given similar year-long scholarships. The others were Charles Eames from St. Louis, Harry Weese from M.I.T., David Scholes from Yale, Henry Hebbeln from Cornell, Ralph Rapson from Michigan, and a South American student named Rodolfo Moore from Argentina.

Very shortly after we arrived at Cranbrook, Saarinen gave a talk, telling us that we were in a place with very unusual facilities, with teachers who were tops in their fields and well-equipped studios for doing all kinds of crafts—metalwork, ceramics, weaving, and carpentry. He said he hoped we, the planners and architects, would take advantage of this set-up to experiment in some of these different fields of design. Everyone seemed to take this to heart; the architects spent most of their year potting and weaving and doing metalwork—very little city planning got done. Of the architects, I think I was the only one who actually did some work in planning, thanks to Walter C. Behrendt, whom I had gotten to know when he lectured at Princeton. Behrendt was head of the Buffalo City-Planning Association, and he very kindly offered to let me come to Buffalo and spend some time working in his office on the Buffalo Waterfront Development. Thus it happened that I spent a miserably cold couple of months in Buffalo. I mostly remember the high piles of snow on each side of the sidewalks.

The Cranbrook campus was a luxurious and beautiful place. Each of us had his own studio, and we were not on any kind of schedule. We had no responsibilities whatever as far as the school was concerned. If we wanted advice or criticism from Saarinen, or "Pappy," as he was called by the students, we could ask for it and he would give it. Otherwise, we didn't have to see him at all if we didn't want to. But there was a lot of activity in the studios. Marianne Strengell was teaching weaving, and Harry Bertoia metalwork. Wallace Mitchell was assistant teacher in painting and drawing under Zoltan Sepeshy, and Carl Milles was head of the sculpture department. An extraordinary woman from Finland, Maija Grotell, was teaching pottery. Eero Saarinen was also in residence, having come back to Cranbrook to work with his father and his brother-in-law, Bob Swanson. Eero's mother and his sister Pipsan, who was married to Swanson, were both involved in weaving projects.

Clockwise from top left Silver and pewter mint-julep cups, made while I was at Cranbrook. Three folding looms designed and built by me and Harry Weese (seated at he looms are myself, Harry, and Wally Mitchell). Eero Saarinen, Eliel Saarinen, Walter Gropius, Jean Labatut, Richard Hudnut, and Antonin Raymond with model of the Smithsonian Art Gallery. Standing in front of a wall hanging I made from a design by Ray Eames.

Top Eero Saarinen (left) and Charles Eames at Cranbrook. *Bottom* Ray Kaiser at her marriage to Charles Eames in Chicago.

Cranbrook itself was a kind of beautiful never-neverland full of buildings, all in a warm pinkish brick, designed by Eliel Saarinen. Around the entire campus were fountains designed by Carl Milles. Wherever you turned, the place had a strong feeling of architecture and the arts. It was beautifully landscaped and maintained. There was a big irregularly shaped pool for swimming; we used to have picnics sometimes inside the big Milles bronze bowls near the pool or go swimming at night in some of the fountains. It was a very happy year, isolated in this beautiful place with people who were all interested in the arts and all doing creative things.

I did quite a bit of pottery with Maija Grotell and also metalwork, but I found metalwork very hard and had to have a lot of help from Harry Bertoia. I liked the pace and the rhythm of weaving, and, with Marianne Strengell's encouragement, Harry Weese and I designed and built three folding looms. I later made material for two suits and several rugs on one of these. We went to Detroit now and then to attend the symphony, and many interesting people came to lecture on the arts or play music, among them Walter Behrendt's wife, Lydia (who was a concert pianist and specialist in the music of Paul Hindemith), Frank Lloyd Wright, and Walter Gropius.

I spent the summer of 1939 in Alabama but went back to Cranbrook in the fall to work in the office of Eliel and Eero Saarinen and Bob Swanson. I worked mostly on an elaborate model of the Smithsonian Art Gallery, which the Saarinens were designing for the mall in Washington. Harry Bertoia was doing metalwork for the model, making silver railings and window muntins set into Plexiglas, while Carl Milles did special tiny sculptures, including a Pegasus figure in silver for the main reflecting pool. Charlie Eames was the other member of the model team.

The model was very large and made of the actual marble to be used for the building. The roofs were removable and the galleries inside were laid out with exhibitions of paintings. I did hundreds of tiny paintings for Eero's approval, and he was very selective in his choice. This selectivity also applied to the metal trees we made to represent the landscaping around the model. Dozens were submitted and few were accepted. The model was so elaborate that I think the building would have been an anticlimax. But it was never built, being a victim of the war. The model was exhibited in Washington, under the dome of the Capitol, and is now in one of the museums there.

While I was working with the Saarinens, Harry Weese had gone

Top Harry Bertoia (center), Eliel Saarinen, and I looking at the model of the Smithsonian Art Gallery. *Bottom* Chair I made out of flat pieces of plywood (design project at Cranbrook).

Top Marianne Strengell. *Bottom* Some of the glazed pottery I made in the ceramics studio at Cranbrook.

Top Painting instructor Wallace Mitchell, Rita Shacht, and Harry Weese by the swimming pool at Cranbrook. *Bottom* Harry Weese and his Model-T Ford in which we made trips to Chicago.

back to Chicago and was working for Skidmore, Owings and Merrill. After I finished my work with the Saarinens, Harry and I decided to become partners. We chose as our headquarters the Chicago suburb of Kenilworth, where Harry lived with his parents. I found a place to live nearby, a small building in the backyard of a house that belonged to the wife of the architect George Washington Maher.* My quarters consisted of just one room with a bath, no kitchen. I had most of my meals with the Weeses, but Harry and I worked in my room. We did a number of houses, mostly for Harry's relatives, including two houses for aunts of his and one for his parents in Barrington, west of Chicago. This house was on the same property where Harry and his wife Kitty (my sister) later built a house of their own.

In 1940 the Museum of Modern Art in New York held a competition for contemporary furniture design called "Organic Design." We submitted several sheets of designs and won a number of awards, including first place in the outdoor furniture category. Samples of some of the winning designs were made and then exhibited both at the Museum of Modern Art and at Bloomingdale's in their furniture department. Harry and I went to New York for the dinner at the museum and a party at Bloomingdale's. Unfortunately, the war jinxed production of most of the furniture, especially our designs, which were made of metal. The thing that really developed out of this exhibition was the Saarinen-Eames furniture, which was later revised, developed, and put into production.

When the U.S.A. became involved in the Second World War, Harry and I both had fairly low draft numbers, but we went on working on the jobs we were doing. We were both planning to go into the Navy, but Harry was suddenly drafted into the Army. As soon as he got his notice from the draft board, he rushed downtown, enlisted in the Navy, and was assigned to Great Lakes Training Base as a sailor. I saw the handwriting on the wall, and as soon as I could, I went back to Alabama. There I found out that I could get into the Navy as an ensign—they were taking architects into a section called Photographic

Interpretation. I had my physical and filled out all the papers. I was accepted after a short time but then spent several months at a basic training school at Harvard, followed by specialized training in photo interpretation at Anacostia, outside Washington. I was stationed for a short period of time in Norfolk, Virginia, and went overseas at the time of the African invasion with Navy Squadron, VP-92, which had been in Guantanamo.

The squadron flew directly to Casablanca but, along with about a hundred sailors and a few other officers, I sailed from Norfolk on a troop convoy. The convoy arrived in Casablanca harbor on Christmas Eve in 1944. I remember that as we came into the harbor, Bing Crosby was singing "I'm Dreaming of a White Christmas" over the intercom system. At first, we stayed in planes at the French air base since there were no houses or buildings where we could set up headquarters. Eventually we acquired two very nice houses on Anfa Hill, which had been confiscated from their German owners. Casablanca had been occupied by the Germans, and they took most of the available food when they left, so we had very little for a while, until supplies could be rounded up from the docks. The procedure for our acquisitions consisted of driving around in a fork-lift until we found a refrigerator or something else we needed. Then we just hoisted it up, put it in the back of a truck, and drove off with it. Thus we were able to outfit the houses with the most of the necessities.

While we were in Casablanca the Anfa Conference took place. A long and very mysterious ramp was built at the airfield and nobody had any idea what it was for. Finally, we learned that President Roosevelt was coming for the conference, and the ramp had been put up to allow his wheelchair to leave the plane. When the conference started, the whole of Anfa Hill where we had our two houses was ringed with a circle of Army and Navy officers. Many of the top people came for the conference, including Admiral Ernest J. King and Winston Churchill, who used to go down the hill in the evening to play the guitar and sing with the Navy enlisted men.

We weren't able to move around very much, but several members of the photographic department and I made a trip by jeep to Marrakesh, a beautiful city with red earth-color buildings, as opposed to the dead white ones in Casablanca. We also took a trip to Fez and stayed in the Medina in an old palace, which had been converted into a hotel. Right outside the hotel door was an endless maze of covered streets, very narrow and lined with shops of artisans of all kinds.

---

* Maher, George Grant Elmslie, and Frank Lloyd Wright all began their architectural careers in the 1880s in the office of John Silsbee, who specialized in residential work and who served as interior architect for the Potter Palmers' picturesque "castle" on Lake Shore Drive in Chicago. Maher and Wright later worked for the firm of Adler and Sullivan. The Maher house was interesting because he had designed the house and the interior as a single entity. It was a dark, somber place with low ceilings, heavy oak beams and woodwork, and secluded nooks with built-in settees.

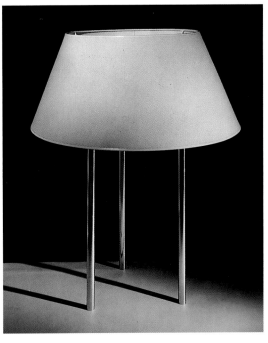

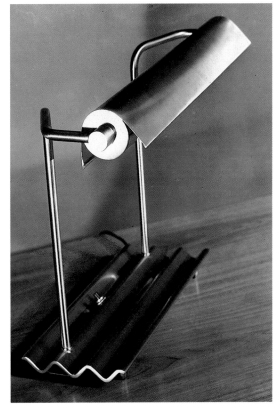

Clockwise from top left Harry Weese (right) and I standing by the teacart that we submitted to the "Organic Design" competition. A three-legged table lamp (submitted in the lighting category of the same show). A desk lamp (also submitted).* Full view of the teacart.

*Baldwin, Benjamin and Weese, Harry M.; Desk Lamp. (1941); Metal, 12¹/₂ in. high x 17 in. wide x 7 in. depth. Mfr.: Mutual Sunset Lamp Mfg. Co., New York, New York, USA. The Museum of Modern Art, New York. Purchase Fund. Photograph © 1995 The Museum of Modern Art, New York.

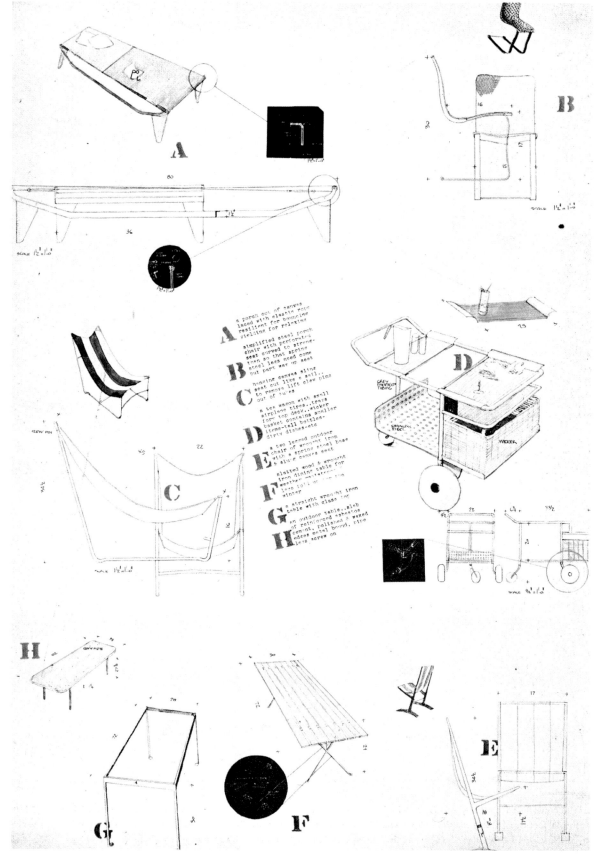

A

B

A a porch cot of canvas
laced with elastic rope
resilient for bouncing
resilient for relaxing
yielding for relaxing

B simplified steel porch
chair with perforated
seat curved to strong-
then so that spring
steel legs need come
but part way up seat

C hanging canvas sling
seat cut like a sail..
to remove lift claw pins
out of tubes

D a tea wagon with small
airplane tires..trays
for top deck..wicker
basket contains smaller
items..tall bottles-
dirty dishes-etc

E a two legged outdoor
chair of wrought iron
with a spring steel base
+ sling canvas seat

F slatted wood & wrought
iron dining table for
weather resistance
here folding up in
winter

G a straight wrought iron
table with glass top

H an outdoor table..slab
of reinforced asbestos
cement, polished + waxed
edges metal bound, tire
legs screw on

C

D

H

G

F

E

Left Sheet of designs (1939) submitted in
the outdoor furniture category of the
"Organic Design" competition. *Below* As
a Navy ensign, Morocco, 1942.

My sister Kitty and Harry Weese at
the time of their marriage.

Once I made a day trip by plane to Algiers, but we were so restricted there as to where we could go that I didn't see very much of the city. Most of the time I had free was spent in Rabat, which was only a short jeep ride away. Despite the shortage of food, in Rabat you could manage to find rather bad meals in one hotel and one or two restaurants.

I made friends with a family of Swedes who had a charming house in Rabat where they had lived for twenty years. They collected antique Moroccan rugs in the Atlas Mountains and other parts of the country and sent them back to France to shops and museums. Their house was behind a high wall and had a lovely inside garden with a little gazelle running free among the plants. I had dinner with them a number of times and sometimes just stopped in to sit in their quiet garden and listen to the fountain. When I left to come back to the States they gave me a beautiful old Moroccan rug. Since I could bring back only one box of gear, I discarded a lot of my Navy equipment and uniforms and brought back the rug, which I still have.

In 1945 I returned to the States in a Navy seaplane. We flew down the coast of Africa to Dakar, then across to Brazil, up along the coast of South America, and finally to Bermuda and New York. Since we flew only during the day and stopped someplace every night, it took about nine days. We were carrying some enlisted men who had been wounded in the Mediterranean as well as a load of mica in boxes. There were no seats in the plane so we sat on the boxes except during take-offs, when we were assigned to specific locations. We had engine trouble when we arrived in Belém and had to spend three days there while repairs were made, so I was able to see at least a small part of Brazil. I spent most of my time at the botanical gardens, which were full of exotic tropical plants I'd never seen before.

When we got back to New York, after what seemed like an endless journey, I had a short leave and then reported to the Navy Department in Washington for my next tour of duty. The city was jammed, and it was difficult to find a place to live. After staying for a while in a friend's house on Dupont Circle, I finally found an apartment nearby. The house was full of women architects, some of whom were working for Eero Saarinen, including Dorothy Noyes and Betty Lundquist, who was a photographer. They were all afraid to live on the ground floor of the house so it was empty, and I promptly moved in. I had no furniture so I bought a bed and made some makeshift tables with bases of rolled corrugated paper. My housemates helped out with some chairs and a sofa they had relegated to the basement.

The next year was fascinating. At work I got to see all of the action films being sent back from the Pacific. Plus, it seemed to me that everybody I'd ever known was either in Washington or came to visit for one reason or another. Lily and Eero Saarinen were living in a house in Georgetown, and a lot of us gathered there for Sunday breakfasts. Philip Johnson used to come to the house on some weekends. He was stationed at an Army base in Virginia and was designing a house on the Potomac in his free time, using one of the drafting boards upstairs. John Johansen was working in Washington as were several of the young architects who afterwards formed the Architects' Collaborative in Cambridge with Walter Gropius. One gathering for drinks at my apartment included Eero Saarinen, Serge Chermayeff, Siegfried Gideon, and Dean Hudnut from Harvard, a very high-powered group to say the least.

After a year in Washington, I got out of the Navy and decided I would not go back to Chicago, but returned instead to New York. I settled down in a small apartment in Manhattan in the Murray Hill section, on Lexington Avenue. Then I started looking for a job. After only a short time I ran into Bill Hartmann, who had been one of Harry

Ink sketch done in Morocco.

Joan Miró's original watercolor sketch of his mural for the Terrace Plaza Hotel, made for my cardboard model of the room.

Weese's roommates at M.I.T. and whom I knew slightly. Just out of the Air Corps, he was now with Skidmore, Owings and Merrill in their New York office. He suggested that I come to the office to talk about a job. The firm was just beginning work on the design of the Terrace Plaza Hotel in Cincinnati, and I was hired as designer in charge of interiors for that job. The Skidmore office in New York was then very small, occupying two floors of a narrow building on Fifty-seventh Street between Fifth and Madison avenues. The designers (there were only five or six people in the department) and the big shots were on one floor next to the conference room and the drafting and engineering staffs were on the floor below.

The whole time I was with Skidmore, Owings and Merrill, I worked on the one job in Cincinnati. In addition to the hotel the building had space for two stores, J. C. Penney and Bond. These were on the lower floors with entrances on the street level, while the lobby of the hotel was on the eighth floor. Hotel guests took elevators from an entrance hall on the ground floor up to the reception area in the main lobby. The main dining room was also on this floor, as well as a bar with a large adjoining terrace. Above the lobby floor were the guest rooms and on the very top a small restaurant called the Gourmet Room in a round penthouse cantilevered over the side of the building.

We designed everything that went into the hotel, including the furniture, fabrics, china, matchbooks, and uniforms. I think this was one of the first public buildings in the country to commission contemporary works of art especially for its spaces. Alexander Calder did a large mobile for the main lobby, and Saul Steinberg did an enormous mural for the main dining room. Jim Davis, who had been teaching at Princeton when I was there, did a very interesting mural in the bar out of sheets of Plexiglas painted with transparent colors. This was lit from different angles so that colored shadows and reflections were thrown on the wall behind the bar, moving as the lights changed. Joan Miró did a thirty-foot-long mural for the curved wall behind the banquettes in the Gourmet Room. Marianne Strengell designed printed fabrics for the bedroom curtains. We worked on furniture with the Thonet Company, one of the few companies at that time making anything that looked contemporary.

The interior design team included Jane Kidder, Klaus Grabe, and Natalie DeBlois. Natalie stayed on at Skidmore, became one of the partners, and was in the Chicago office until she retired. Before the job was finished, Dave Allen joined us for a summer. He later became head of the interior design department after I left. Bill Brown was the partner in charge of the project, and Abe Feder was the lighting consultant.

I was still very much interested in painting and sculpture and one of the best things about the job at Skidmore was my contact with the artists who were hired to create the art for the hotel. When Miró came to New York I went to see him at the apartment where he was staying and talked to him about the possibility of doing a design for the mural in the Gourmet Room. I also went to see Pierre Matisse, who was Miró's agent, to discuss the project with him. Saul Steinberg, whom I had known in Washington when we were both in the Navy, made a trip to Cincinnati at the same time that I was out there to see the city; he was planning a sort of bird's-eye view of the city and commentary on life there.

Several times I visited with Calder at his house in Connecticut, a wonderful place in the country with a big studio full of mobiles and stabiles. There were other meetings in New York with Calder and Mr. Skidmore over lunch in the Oak Room at the Plaza Hotel. Calder usually turned up in a bright fireman's-red wool shirt and, after consuming several martinis before lunch, was often very jolly. One day I admired a tie he was wearing, and he told me it was designed and made for him by Jean Lurçat. He said that if I liked it so much he would make me a tie. I replied that I thought that would be wonderful. Calder then said there would be one condition: that I would wear it for ten days after I got it. I agreed and then forgot all about our conversation.

Weeks later a box arrived for me at the office. In it was the tie in all its splendor. Made out of several pieces of bright-colored felt stitched together, it was already tied so all you had to do was slip it over your head and tighten the knot. Down the front Calder had stitched "Ben Baldwin archt." There was a long piece of bathtub chain on the bottom and in the center a multi-colored metal wheel attached so it could spin around. I put the tie in the drawer of my drafting table so it would be easily accessible in an emergency. And an emergency came very soon. Just a few days later I got a call from the secretary saying that I was wanted in the conference room and that Mr. Calder was there for a meeting. So I quickly put on the tie and went to join the session. Mr. Skidmore, Calder, and the clients from Cincinnati were all there when I walked in wearing the creation. Calder exploded with laughter. I still have the tie although I don't often get to wear it.

The Skidmore, Owings and Merrill office was right in the middle of all the best galleries, which were concentrated at that time around Fifty-seventh Street. I spent many of my lunch hours going to see various exhibitions. Because I had always loved Paul Klee, one of my favorite galleries was Nierendorf's, the sole agent in New York for Klee's work. Mr. Nierendorf would let me spend time in his apartment above the gallery where I could pull out all the Klees and stand them against the walls of the living room.

I still have a list of watercolors and oils that I was considering buying. The prices look pretty amazing now—beautiful paintings for a hundred and fifty to two hundred dollars. My salary at Skidmore was about two hundred dollars a week, which was a lot at that time, and whatever I saved was invested in art. I bought an early Klee watercolor and an oil called *Old Married Couple,* then one of the most beautiful of all the oils called *Woman's Mask,* and, finally, the best of all, one of the magic squares series called *New Harmony.* One of the largest paintings Klee did, the last work is now in the Guggenheim Museum. Later on I added a beautiful drawing to my collection.

Once, coming down in the elevator from one of the Klee exhibitions, I met Ward Bennett and we started talking. We became good friends and have been ever since. At that time Ward was making sculpture and heavy brass jewelry, and I was able to get him involved in the hotel project. He made some large brass circles with cut-outs in them which we used as light baffles in the cocktail area outside the Gourmet Room.

After the war ended, the office began to expand very rapidly to handle the amount of postwar building that was cropping up. About this time Gordon Bunshaft was moved from the Chicago office to the New York office, and Bill Hartmann became head of the office in Chicago. I could see that the Skidmore office was going to become a large operation, and I proposed to them that the interior design function be set up as a separate entity. My proposal was not approved, and so I decided I would rather work on my own. My life as an independent designer had begun.

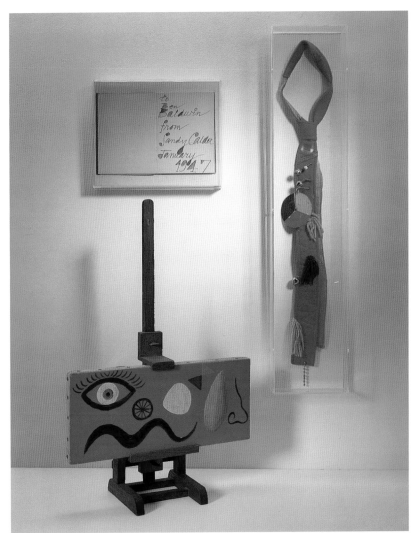

Top Note from Calder that accompanied the tie he made for me. *Bottom* Mounted on the easel is a painting by Alexander Calder, given to me when he was making a mobile sculpture for the Terrace Plaza Hotel Lobby; in the cases are Calder's note and the tie.

The Roofs Over My Head

The Roofs Over My Head

After leaving Skidmore, Owings and Merrill, I started looking for a place where I could both live and set up my own design office. This established a pattern I was to follow throughout my years as a designer. I have always resisted the idea of a big office and have chosen to work on a small, selective scale, living and working under the same roof. This has advantages and disadvantages. You don't have to go out in the rain and snow to get to work, but clients and contractors take advantage of your being available after normal working hours.

The ideal location came along very soon. Dorothy Noyes, whom I had known in Washington at the end of the war, was about to start a shop for modern furnishings called New Design and had found a five-story brownstone on Seventy-fifth Street just east of Madison Avenue, opposite the present location of the Whitney Museum. She wanted somebody to lease the house with her, so I decided to join her and take the two top floors. The shop would occupy the basement and first floor, and she would live on the second floor. We signed the lease, and I started on the first of a long series of remodelings aimed at converting miserable, chopped-up rooms into simple, liveable architectural spaces.

The large square room in front on the top floor faced south and was flooded with sunshine as there were no tall buildings opposite. The three windows facing the street were recessed and had natural wood shutters which had never been painted and worked perfectly. I was happy with this as I have never liked curtains in my own apartments and houses. This room was to be living room and workroom.

But first the stairwell had to be enclosed and after that a fin wall extended to enclose a long desk surface over which I built bookshelves. There was no provision for lighting other than convenience outlets so adjustable ceiling fixtures were installed to wash the walls with light. The plaster was very bad on the fireplace wall so it was all stripped off exposing the bare bricks, an approach which later became a cliché.

The furnishings were in keeping with the minimal space: a metal cot frame with mattress, which served as a sofa; an original Hardoy chair with a natural leather sling seat; two high-back camp chairs from Gold Medal covered in black and white calfskin; and a three-legged desk chair designed by Charles Eames. This last item had a stained red seat and back and had been designed for the Museum of Modern Art's "Organic Design" competition but was never put in production. Charles made me a gift of this one. There were also two plow-seat stools of my own design that I had made especially for this apartment. As far as I know this was the first use of a plow seat for seating other than on a tractor.

Art has always played an important part in my interiors and this room was no exception. On the fireplace wall hung Klee's beautiful magic squares oil, *New Harmony.* Over the built-in desk was an early Klee watercolor, *Composition with Houses,* and a stone *Woman with Child* by the primitive sculptor Will Edmondson of Nashville, Tennessee.

The L-shaped room in the back served as bedroom and dining room, with a kitchenette arrangement built into one leg of the L. The bathroom was in the center between the bedroom and the front workroom. The floor below, which was also mine, had two similarly sized rooms which were in very good condition. Each of these had a bath, so I decided to rent these to friends. The larger front room was rented to Edward Barnes, who had his first office there. At that time he was working alone with one draftsman. The back room was rented to Dale Bird, who was doing renderings for Skidmore, Owings and Merrill and for Marcel Breuer.

About this time Ward Bennett and I decided to take exercise classes with José Limón's dance group, and we joined the class for beginners. Bill Machado, who had been studying painting and dancing, joined the exercise class a short time later. He and I became good friends and a few months later decided to join forces at Seventy-fifth Street. He had not trained as an architect or designer but had been doing painting, so we decided to design a line of printed fabrics, since this seemed to be something we could work on together. We called our joint venture Design Unit New York and operated under that name while we were on Seventy-fifth Street. We produced a line of printed fabrics which was distributed for several years by Arundell Clarke. A number of our designs were exhibited at the Museum of Modern Art, and one of them, called "Barrel Heads," was used in the

Bill Machado and I in my apartment
on East 75th Street, New York.

East Seventy-fifth Street, New York

View from the entrance into the living-workroom.

Top left A sketch I made of the kitchenette. *Bottom left* Storage wall of living-workroom room. *Below* The bedroom. The storage units are covered by sliding panels on light wood frames; the seat is covered with a yellow cotton rug I wove at Cranbrook; on the shelves are an ink drawing by Hugo Weber and a watercolor by Miro.

model house designed by Marcel Breuer and built in the garden of the museum. They were also shown in several other museums and published in a number of magazines devoted to design and interiors.

During this period I was not involved in very much architecture or interior design, although I did design a house for my mother, which was built in Montgomery, Alabama. Harry Weese's brother, John, who was also in New York, worked with me on the drawings and specifications. He later became a partner in the San Francisco office of Skidmore, Owings and Merrill. I was, however, quite active in the art world. As New York representative for the California magazine *Arts and Architecture*, I wrote articles on different painters, and this provided me with a connection to this world that I might not otherwise have had. The New York School was flourishing, and we got to know a number of these artists, who sometimes gathered at our apartment in the evening for drinks. The group included William Baziotes, Adolph Gottlieb, Mark Rothko, Robert Motherwell, Theodore Stamos, Barnett Newman, Herbert Ferber, and Franz Kline. I had also gotten to know Arshile Gorky right after I came back to New York from the Navy. He was staying a lot of the time out in Sherman, Connecticut, at Henry Hebbeln's farm. Henry and his wife Jean had both been at Cranbrook when I was there, and I often went to their place in Sherman for weekends.

There were still wonderful galleries, run by dealers who were really dedicated, concentrated around Fifty-seventh Street. I added several good pictures to my small collection. I bought two beautiful Gorky drawings from a show at Julian Levy's gallery and a gouache, a drawing, and an oil by Hans Hofmann from Peggy Guggenheim's Art of This Century, an interesting gallery designed by Frederick Kiesler, one room of which had concave walls. My other favorite galleries were Betty Parsons and the Willard Gallery. Marion Willard had beautiful exhibitions of Morris Graves and Mark Tobey and the first exhibitions I remember of Richard Pousette-Dart's paintings and Richard Lippold's wire sculptures. Lippold and I became friends, and I remember going with him to a special evening at John Cage's studio in Lower Manhattan. Richard had done two new wire sculptures which were installed at Cage's apartment. John did a musical celebration in honor of these sculptures in a bare room where we sat on the floor.

In 1947 Bill Machado and I decided to move to Alabama. After spending a short time in an apartment, we bought a dilapidated house on Adams Street in the same block with the capitol and the

Clockwise from top left Bedroom of Marcel Breuer's house in the garden of the Museum of Modern Art; Baldwin-Machado fabric "Barrel Heads" on bed covers. Bill Machado and I looking at fabric design. "Jack Straws" at window and "Spools" on table. "Starry Pines" on natural silk. "Carnival (color version). "Carnival" (line version). "Barrel Heads."

Adams Street, Montgomery

State Archives Building. So I was back again where I had started, right beside the capitol of the Confederacy. It was an L-shaped house, wood frame, and all the windows were missing. It had simple details and good proportions, and we liked the location. So we bought the place for very little and started remodeling. We added a new front porch to replace one that had collapsed, keeping the original entrance door with glass over the top and on both sides. Through this door you entered a small hallway with a square room on the left, which we used as a workroom, and on the right were two small rooms, which we combined into one living room; behind this was a bedroom. We kept the original double-hung windows in these rooms, except on the side toward the inside courtyard. Here we installed large windows of fixed glass and doors opening out onto a deck. The deck connected the front hall to the kitchen in the addition that we built at the back of the house. This addition made the house U-shaped around the inside courtyard and provided a new bath and a tall screened porch in addition to the kitchen. The house stood on piers several feet off the ground and the screened porch was at ground level, so there were steps from the kitchen down onto the porch. We made a small garden with a fountain inside the courtyard and another behind the new wing. Most of the back garden we paved with brick, but there was a long planting bed with *Fatsia japonica,* several kinds of bamboo, and other tropical-looking plants.

One of our main reasons for going back to Alabama was that I would be able to use Kintray, which was standing empty and unused. Also I was curious to see what living in Alabama would be like and whether or not we could make a go of working there. Most of our work during this period was interior design, although I did design a building downtown on Dexter Avenue for John Danziger—a store for ladies' clothes. My family owned the building, which had been almost completely destroyed by fire. The place was gutted, so we designed a completely new building. I also designed a house quite similar to the one I had done earlier for my mother. The new one was in brick rather than wood, but the layouts were similar. Finally, I did a group of several houses for Pascal Shook in a small development he was promoting on the outskirts of Birmingham.

Our interior design projects included Henrietta and Pascal Shook's own house in Birmingham, a vacation house at the Gulf, a house in Chapman, Alabama, for Betty and Julian McGowin (designed by Hugh Jackson), and a number of apartments and houses in and around Montgomery. After we had been at Adams Street about a year, we decided to open a downtown shop and interior design office in a building that belonged to my family. At first we had a large space upstairs with an entrance from the street into a small hall and up a steep stairway. We concentrated on contemporary furniture, furnishings, and fabrics. But apparently we were too far ahead of Montgomery's thinking at the time, and we did not do very well. The next year we moved downstairs into half of the space on the first floor, but the shop was still not a success.

Certainly the thing I enjoyed most about the time we spent in Alabama was being near Kintray. In 1931, when I was a freshman at Princeton, my father had died, followed a year later by my grandfather, and I inherited Kintray. The whole family went on using Kintray. During our college years it was still very much a center of activity in our lives, particularly in the summers when we were all in Alabama, and we invited friends to share the place with us. It was then that I made some changes in the general character of the interior of the house, mostly in the way of simplification, trying to eliminate all of the things that seemed to detract from the space and real function of the place. I took down all the stuffed fish and animal heads and the reproductions of paintings in the Link and the front hall and brought in my own collection of contemporary paintings—things I had bought over the years since I was in college. I also mixed in some contemporary furniture and recovered the existing furniture in cheerful fabrics, making the Link a comfortable country room.

It is not easy to describe the very special quality of Kintray and what it has meant to me throughout my life. The first thing that comes to mind is the excitement I felt every time I arrived there, coming around the driveway through the woods, around the curves to the top of the hill where the house sat, getting out of the car, stepping onto the big porch, and going into the still, cool house—so quiet and full of wonder. There were always birds singing, accompanied by the lovely sounds of the pine trees and the water down in Chestnut Creek. In the summer it was always much cooler than in the city, and you felt a kind of wonderful relief in this protective and secluded place. It was a place where you could be yourself and do exactly what you felt like doing. There was no need to do anything you felt was being imposed on you or that you didn't really enjoy.

The house was beautifully designed as a summer place. The size of the rooms, the height of the ceilings, the windows coming right

Left View from the deck into the tall screened porch off the kitchen. *Below* Living room with three-legged Scandinavian chairs, custom-made slat table, dining table, sofa, and end table; antique revolving bookcase in corner; paintings by Paul Klee and Robert Motherwell. The adjustable dining light has a wooden acorn as a weight.

Kintray, Verbena, Alabama

down to the floor, the wide porches, the great attic spaces over the house, and the vast overhangs beyond the porches all made it a very comfortable house for the Alabama summer climate.

The rooms were full of light and air and generous in size. I tried to emphasize these qualities by taking out as many of the junky things as possible. The furniture had never been anything very special. Most of what was in the house when my grandparents lived there was oak, and there were very few interesting antiques. Once I had simplified the place as much as I could, the pieces of modern furniture and the paintings I'd collected were very much at home with the old pieces I did keep.

It would have been too vast an undertaking to try to change the architecture, even on the inside of the house. It was too large and too set in its ways. I didn't even paint the large rooms but left them exactly as they were, concentrating on the small rooms in the back of the house. Here I had almost no furniture, white walls, straw matting, and a few paintings. I turned the servants' house into a studio and put a big window in one of the rooms. I used this as an extra place for working, painting, or making models.

As far as gardening is concerned, my parents and grandparents had always had a large vegetable garden and many fruit trees, which provided us with peaches, pecans, strawberries, and all kinds of vegetables. When I took over Kintray, I turned an area outside one end of the Link into a garden and made a hedge along one side with some transplanted native cedars. I bought some large boxwood bushes from a lady in the country near Verbena and had them transplanted to this garden. The area had originally been my grandmother's rose garden, but this was too precious for me and, in any case, most of her rose bushes had died. So I concentrated on flowering shrubs and some perennials. Close to the Link there were clumps of tiger lilies. I kept these and planted a lot of bamboo just beyond them around the kitchen and pantries. Bamboo has always been my favorite plant.

I never tried to make a very extensive garden at Kintray, partly because the woods and natural surroundings were so beautiful in themselves. I enjoyed working outside, but it was always enough work just to keep the weeds more or less under control and to keep the place as clean as possible. I didn't have a Sullivan, who used to get up very early every morning and mop the entire front porch in my grandfather's day. I had learned that change is the only thing one can count on.

View from the Link looking into the back hall. The wicker armchair is old, the other chair is a contemporary piece from Mexico; the rosewood table, above which hangs a Chinese bamboo lantern, was made from an old square piano; the ink-colored crayon drawing is by Hans Hofmann.

Above The living end of the Link with an upright Steinway piano, Mexican chairs, my Cranbrook loom, and a bent plywood table by Alvar Aalto. *Far left* Armchair of bent bamboo, designed by Charlotte Perriand, made in Japan. *Left* Screened tennis court shelter supported on stumps of trees.

Top The Link. The oversize seat was ideal for reading or napping; the painting is by Bill Traylor. *Bottom* My bedroom in the old part of the house.

On the mantel are sculptor's tools; the floor lamp was one of the Weese-Baldwin designs submitted to the "Organic Design" competition.

Our life in Alabama was very pleasant. Besides the comforts of Kintray, we were also quite near the Gulf of Mexico and could drive down to Fort Walton or Destin in a few hours. I have always loved this area with its endless white sand beaches, crystal clear blue-green water, low dunes with dwarf magnolia trees, and ancient live oaks. We spent many happy weekends at Destin in a little rented house perched on top of the dunes looking out over the Gulf. The whole area has been built up now with motels and condominiums.

Very few people in Alabama were interested in contemporary design, and my sister Kitty, who owned a shop for contemporary furnishings in Chicago with a designer friend of hers named Jody Kingrey, kept suggesting that Bill Machado and I move to Chicago and use the shop Baldwin Kingrey as our base of operations. We finally decided to do this and put our house in town up for sale. I went to Chicago in 1955 and found an apartment on East Ontario Street, very near the shop, and Bill joined me there a short time later. The apartment was nothing special. The entrance was opposite the bathroom with the living room and a kitchen-dining alcove to the right and a bedroom and another small room to the left. The apartment's best assets were its high ceiling and good wood floors. Since this was a temporary situation, we made no real changes in the place. We kept the Victorian white marble mantel and the stained wood floors in the living room, using the rug from the Atlas Mountains that I had brought home from my Navy tour of Morocco. A seven-foot-long custom-made sofa, backed by industrial steel bookshelves, an Aalto coffee table in natural birch, two Danish basket chairs with teak frames, and an armless sofa in black horsehair made up the furnishings—a very simple setting for my Klees and primitive art.

In the beginning, we had our work quarters at Baldwin Kingrey, and our first clients in Chicago were customers of the shop. As we began to get more work, we took an office on the ground floor of a building on Erie Street, directly behind our apartment. We shared this with an architect friend, Richard Barringer.

This office had just two rooms—a large one with a bay window on the street and a smaller room just large enough for two drafting tables and a lot of shelves for samples and reference material. It was all painted white, with cocoa matting on the painted concrete floors. The wall separating the two rooms had two round-headed arches behind which we mounted sliding panels of Guatemalan cotton in four colors. Each panel consisted of two colors of cotton sewn together in a

The dining end of the Link. The drop light over the table was made from a plow disk found in the barn.

Ontario Street, Chicago

The apartment in summer dress, with two thick tatami mats and a big rope hammock by the windows. In the steel bookshelves is an Ogowe River (Gabon) dance mask.

zig-zag pattern. A folding screen divided the larger room into reception and conference areas. In the reception area was a Danish sofa in
black cotton, two antique oval-back armchairs, and custom-made
walnut tables with white marble tops. The conference area contained
six very simple Victorian chairs in black lacquer and a custom-made
Formica-topped table on a black restaurant base.

In 1957 Bill Machado moved back to Alabama to live and work.
A short time after this I found a house I liked on North State Street
near the Ambassador Hotel and decided to buy it and once again
combine my working and living quarters under one roof. The house
was one of an identical pair, which were attached but reversed in plan.
The outside walls were soft Indiana limestone with wood trim and a
wood bay window. I kept the color of the stone and had the wood
parts painted a dark putty green. Behind the house was a deep, narrow yard with one mock orange tree and a lot of cinders. I set about
right away to make this into a garden. I added a wood deck onto the
back of the house with three steps going down to a walk of concrete
squares. Beyond this was a wide area of tiny gravel, bordered all
around the edges by bricks. At the center point of this gravel area I
made a shallow reflecting pool with a jet of water. The bottom and
edges of the pool were of the same brick as the borders of the plant
beds. On the south side of the garden was a low wood fence that belonged to the garden next door, and along this fence I made a narrow
planting bed. On the opposite side, I placed a wider planting bed with
a higher fence behind it. This I covered with Dutchman's pipe to block
out the rather unattractive building on that side. I stuffed the plant
beds full of perennials, iris, phlox, lilies, pinks, and bulbs. At the back
end of the garden I put up a high wood fence against which were
planted espaliered pear trees. Behind the fence I left an area off the alley deep enough for my car. The garden received sun all day long and
flourished. It was a great treat having this quiet refuge in the heart of
the city. If I walked out the back gate it was just two blocks to the lake.

The entrance to the house led into a hall with a stair going up to
the second and third floors. Immediately to the right of the entrance
was a wide opening into the living room with its fireplace and a bay
with two windows that overlooked the street. Sliding doors connected the living room to the dining room behind it, which also had a
fireplace and a single window onto the back yard. Both rooms had
high ceilings, plastered walls with simple moldings, and wood floors
which I stained dark. I removed the wall with the sliding doors and

State Street, Chicago

Left The bay window overlooking the street. *Below* View of the garden looking toward the house.

made one large space out of these two rooms. The opening from the living room into the hall was closed and, at a point behind the stairs, a new door opened from the hall into the dining end of the room. Both mantels were removed and both fireplaces raised off the floor; the one in the living area only slightly, but the one in the dining area up to the height of the dining table. Both fireplace openings were fitted with fireglass panels set in chrome frames.

I took out the big double-hung window on the garden side of the dining room and installed a greenhouse window about two feet deep, which I filled with green plants. In the dining area I placed my great-grandfather's large oak table. Without any of its leaves it made a square, and I pushed it up against the wall, with the top right under the metal and glass door of the raised fireplace. The table was treated as a library table and was covered with art books, flowers, and objects. I designed a big wing chair covered in natural leather for one side and found a beautiful old bentwood settee and two armchairs, all stained a cherry red color, for the other sides, at Richard Camp in New York.

In the living area I built an L-shaped platform twelve inches high. This was narrow along the wall opposite the fireplace and wide where it cut across the width of the room, where the living and dining areas met. The seat cushion on the wide part was upholstered in olive green brocade and there were cushions to lean back on. The narrow arm of the platform held pictures, flowers, and books. I had bought a reclining Corbusier chair in Switzerland from Heide Webber's shop, and this was placed by the fireplace. It was in zebra skin and really handsome. Some years later these chairs were imported to the States and made available to designers. Two oval-back armchairs that I had designed myself worked well as pull-up chairs.

The hallway of the house originally led all the way back to the kitchen, which had windows onto the back yard. I converted the back part of this hall into a small compact kitchen and made the original kitchen a guest room/sitting room with a place for dining when there were only a few people. There was a door from this room out onto the wood deck. I added new fixtures, including a stall shower, to what had been the powder room, and this became the guest bath. The second floor of the house had a bright sunny sitting room in the front facing south, my workroom in the center of the house, and my bedroom in the back, overlooking the garden. The third floor I made into a separate apartment with a roof deck, but I used it only for guests.

The garden in summer.

Below The living area. The transparent divider between living and dining areas was made of weighted cord which could be tied in various arrangements. *Right* The dining room.

48

Top The second-floor sitting room.
Bottom Guest room/sitting room.

In spite of the fact that I never felt I really belonged in Chicago, I enjoyed the years I spent there. The winters were certainly alien to my Southern blood, but the city had its attractions—the Art Institute, a few good galleries, and the Chicago Symphony. It was an energetic and alive city and an exciting place to work. I enjoyed my house and living two blocks from the lake, making it easy for me to take walks along the water and in the parks nearby. I had made many wonderful friends, but I missed New York, and I decided to move back there again.

I wanted to have a view of trees and sky and be able to walk in pleasant surroundings, so I looked at several apartment buildings on Central Park West, including the Dakota on Seventy-second Street. My friend Ward Bennett had bought a studio on the roof and had converted it into a truly beautiful place to live. I found an apartment there with a view over Central Park which had good possibilities for remodeling, but the gloomy vibrations I got from the building prevented me from signing the contract. In July 1963 I bought an apartment further south, at Sixty-seventh Street and Central Park West.

I enjoyed doing this apartment as much as anything I've ever done. I was my own client and had only myself to please and accommodate. I was starting a new part of my life and wanted the place where I lived and worked to be very special. I was lucky to have Earl Pope doing the working drawings and to find a good contractor. The building was old, which was an advantage in some ways. Tenants were allowed to change windows and remove inside walls as long as they made no structural changes. The windows in the main rooms had already been changed by a former tenant and were quite acceptable. Air conditioners had already been put through the walls beneath them. The location and outlook were superb. My apartment was on the northeast corner of the building, on the ninth floor. There was a Christian Science church to the north of me, and I had a view of the park across its green copper domes from every window on the north side. It was like living in Rome. The windows on the east, in the living room and master bedroom, looked out over the trees to the whole stretch of Fifth Avenue and Central Park South. The place was flooded with morning sunshine and the buildings on Fifth Avenue were washed in gold at sunset. The full moon rose directly in front of my windows, and at Thanksgiving the huge animal balloons of the Macy's parade floated by right outside.

To make the spaces as free-flowing as possible, I took out all of

Central Park West, New York

Dining in the workroom/study at night.

In the workroom/study. The built-in shelf with recessed incandescent light above provides a counter for buffet suppers. The large painting/collage is by Skifano; in the bookshelves are two Giacometti pencil drawings and an ink drawing by Hans Hofmann; the collage hung low on the wall panel is by Le Corbusier.

Above The living room. *Right* Plan of remodeled apartment showing how spaces were opened to flow together.

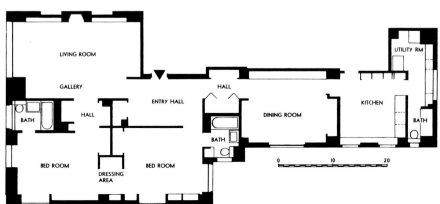

Far left The recessed niche in the living room. The small picture is *Morning Glories* by Braque; on the panel at left is a Hans Hofmann drawing in ink and colored crayon. *Above* The big window and window seat (a subway grill covers the radiators below) look out over Central Park; the large ink painting is by Nell Blaine. *Left* Cushions on window seat.

Left View from the living room into entry hall at left and the hall into the master bedroom at right. *Below* The storage element dividing the master bedroom from the guest room with lighted niche at the end. Oil painting on far wall of guest room is by Hans Hofmann; bedcovers are brown wool.

Left The workroom/study used for
dining. A Le Corbusier collage hangs
to the left of the window and a large
collage/painting by Skifano in the
service niche. *Above* Setting for a
small supper in the hallway in front
of a large painting by Robert Natkin
called *The Bridge*. Amber Venini vase
holds orange lilies; custom-made
Venetian candle cups; blue and white
owl pitcher by Picasso.

Top View from dressing room into master bedroom. Painting next to the window is by Morris Graves. *Bottom* Master bedroom looking into living room with pivot door open flush with wall. Custom-made bedside chest has a pull-out drawer containing the telephone; on the easel is a small painting by Miró.

Below The kitchen with the table set for tea.

the inside walls except those around the two main bathrooms. In the entrance hall, the doors were removed and the space opened into the living room on one side and the study on the other. To emphasize the architecture of the space as much as possible, seats were built into both ends of the room—a platform for sofa cushions at the end where you entered and a window seat at the east end. The entire place was carpeted in undyed beige wool carpet, which went over the platform and up the wall behind it. This was a great help with the acoustics and made the space seem larger. The platform seat and back cushions were mouse-colored linen velvet, while the channeled window-seat cushions were made of natural linen with natural leather edges. These cushions were designed so that two of them rolled up at the ends, forming bolsters.

The moveable furniture was kept to a minimum—two of my oval-back armchairs and some big tufted armchairs in natural leather which Ward Bennett was just beginning to make for Brickel. The bases of these chairs were made to swivel, which added to the flexibility of the arrangement. All of the doors in the apartment were floor to ceiling and folded back into recessed pockets in the walls. They were suspended on pivots in the floor and ceiling and had Formica pushplates and recessed pulls where needed. The jumble of closets between the two bedrooms was too small to use and was redesigned into ample closets with floor-to-ceiling doors. The space next to the outside wall was made into a small dressing room with full-length mirrors, storage unit with shelves hidden behind doors, and a recessed counter-top. Bi-fold doors on the guest-room side of this space could be used to close off the room or could be folded completely flat into the wall, opening the space between the two rooms.

The old dining room, to the left of the entrance hall, became my study and was used for dining in the evening as well. I could sit at my desk and look at the trees in Central Park. I think that in small apartments rooms used only for dining are wasted space, so here I built in bookshelves as well as a long shelf with recessed lighting where I could display art and flowers. The kitchen was also completely redone with a whole wall of floor-to-ceiling storage; a dining table and some of my oval-back chairs were added, making a pleasant and comfortable spot for having breakfast or lunch. I hung some good pictures on the walls, so it became a place I enjoyed. What had been the maid's room was opened into the kitchen, and the refrigerator located there.

Eventually I was asked to redo the lobby of the building by the committee in charge of such things, and this was good luck for me, as the lobby became a sort of extension of my own apartment. I put up two beautiful silk screens from Matisse's *Jazz* series which I wish I had kept!

In the fall of 1965 I decided to sell my apartment, buy property in East Hampton, where I could spend time and work in a pleasant, comfortable atmosphere, and take a smaller apartment in the city. Back in the 1940s, I had had a ground-floor sublet in a brownstone on East Fifty-first Street and had liked the location, so I looked again in that area. Through friends I heard of a place in the same block and went to have a look. I was depressed to say the least. The average New York apartment seems planned to make the occupant unhappy. Architecturally, it is usually a collected clutter of spaces that do not work, clumsy details, impossible lighting, and worn-out equipment. As rents go higher, the amenities provided seem to go down to a sub-minimum. But I thought the place had possibilities and decided to confront the landlord. He was not prepared to spend a cent on the apartment but agreed to give me a five-year lease and his permission to make whatever changes I wanted to make, at my expense, of course. He was trying to encourage architects and designers to move into the building, knowing they would feel it imperative to make improvements. So I signed the lease, found a contractor through an architect friend, and started demolition again.

The first thing to be done was to create one large space out of the living room and the two halls, so the wall between the two halls came down. Then, as it seemed better to have the living room space flow into the kitchen and benefit by the extra window there, the wall between the living room and the kitchen was also removed. I replaced part of this with a plywood storage wall with a recessed shelf and niche on the living room side and low storage with space above for hanging utensils on the kitchen side. I built out the walls around the windows to conceal the different-sized columns and create a recessed space for the radiator. I then hung a blind flush with the wall, concealing the radiator. The worn-out kitchen sink, stove, and refrigerator were all removed and replaced by a Murphy kitchen unit in black. Open shelves above this and on the adjoining wall provided adequate storage for utensils and equipment, since I planned to do a minimum amount of cooking in the apartment.

In the living space, the removal of walls at the entrance exposed beams that ran in a different direction and were a different size from those in the larger space, so I decided to drop the ceiling above the area I planned to use for a conference/dining table. This lowered ceiling at the entrance gave importance to the two larger spaces on each side of it. By continuing the low ceiling and the walls enclosing the old dumbwaiter and the bath into the back room, I created a space for a sculpture niche and shelves for books, pictures, hi-fi equipment, and such. The walls were dropped down in front of the beams and above the windows to the line of this dropped ceiling in both the living space and the work space, tying the whole area together visually and creating a sense of order.

The other major changes in the living area were the addition along one wall of a storage element housing a Murphy bed with recessed shelves next to it; a deep closet where the shallow coat closet had been; and a cabinet full of shelves for clothes and linen. A door with piano hinges went from the floor to the height of the dropped ceiling. The walls enclosing the dumbwaiter had to be left intact, but the projection of this element into the dining space created a niche where the fire door was located. I covered the whole door wall with a white Temlite blind like those at the windows and put in a removable wood shelf for my two favorite Venini vases. I had a collage by Le Corbusier in a deep wood frame, and this worked perfectly as a cover for the intercom phone, which could not be moved. The frame was attached to the wall with a piano hinge so the cover could be easily opened.

Although it was just two spaces with a bath and a kitchen, the apartment's location was convenient to the places I had to go to shop for clients, and there were good restaurants nearby. Installing the Murphy bed in the storage wall of the living room allowed the bedroom to be converted to a workroom with space for a drafting table and a deep closet for work storage. Building platforms for seating in the living room gave this space an architectural, uncluttered look and made it seem larger. An old high-back leather armchair and a telescope lamp from Italy provided a good place to read. Now I could give up my apartment on Central Park West and get on with a house in East Hampton.

In the summer of 1965 I rented a house in Amagansett so I could look for property to buy in or near East Hampton. I had been going to visit friends in the area off and on since the mid-1940s and had come to feel that this was where I would like to have my permanent base of operations. In those days, before the Long Island Expressway

Living room. The cushion on the freestanding platform is covered in Greek blue and white striped wool, the bolster in natural glove leather; table is a bronze Siamese drum. Artworks include a Le Corbusier collage in niche, a Giacometti pencil drawing by window, and two colored drawings by Arshile Gorky over platform.

Right Cover of intercom (framed Le Corbusier collage) shown open. *Below top* Dining area. *Below bottom* The workroom. A painting of three eggs by Charles Shannon and a fiber mask from New Guinea are on shelves; a black mask with tusks from the Ivory Coast is in the small niche.

brought the hordes of weekend tourists and summer renters, East Hampton was a quiet, peaceful village. The two-lane approach to the town passed through peach orchards, duck farms, and fields of potatoes.

I contacted a few real estate agents and started making the rounds, but I found my property completely by accident. I had made an appointment with an agent who lived right in the village, and we started off from her place with a big bunch of keys to all the houses she planned to show me. Very near her house we passed a wooden gate with a very small "For Sale" sign and I asked about it. She said the property had been for sale for years and had sat there neglected. I asked her to stop the car, and we walked up the driveway. I knew instantly it was the place for me.

The part for sale was just under an acre and felt like some ancient romantic ruin. The acre I was walking around had once been the site of a big wooden house that belonged to one of East Hampton's grander residents, Mrs. Lorenzo E. Woodhouse, and was part of a much larger estate that included a sizeable garage, greenhouse, gardener's cottage, and private theatre. The house, designed by Joseph Greenleaf Thorp and built in 1903-04, had been torn down years before I came along, leaving only the brick-walled basement. This was now overgrown with dead vines and small trees that sprouted from the cracked concrete floors. The property had been divided into several pieces; the theatre and the garage had been converted into dwellings and part of the land given to the village as a nature preserve.

The brick piers that had supported the wide front porch were still standing, as was a double row of concrete columns, part of a trellised walk from the back entrance of the house to the garage and greenhouse behind. There was an ancient rusted furnace in one corner of the basement, and the walls were cracked and missing bricks in places. At one end, above the T-shaped foundation, was a concrete terrace which had been covered with tiles, but most of them were missing. On one side in the back of the property there were traces of what must have been a handsome formal garden. A herringbone brick walk led through yew hedges to a high stuccoed wall with a door leading under a rustic arbor to the old greenhouse. In the center of the space were two round pools; in one of these was the broken base of a white marble fountain which I imagined as a bowl with a jet of water in the center. The yew hedges circled around these pools and continued on to a small arbor supported by two concrete pillars.

Huntting Lane, East Hampton

Below top Double row of concrete columns that once supported a trellis.
Below bottom The ruins of the old basement, later converted into a sunken garden.

Tall, stately cypress trees outlined the garden on two sides, while the other side was closed in by dogwood trees. The trees and shrubs had been neglected, and there were tangles of vines and dead branches everywhere.

The asking price was high for the time, and the owner had a long list of restrictions which had to be met, some of which were unreasonable. But the location had everything I wanted: it was the right size, faced south, and was convenient to the village. The landscape had potential. There were some superior trees and rhododendrons around the perimeter as well as some beautiful things put in by Mrs. Woodhouse's English gardener. One of the greatest assets was a huge dogwood tree in the center of the driveway circle. A great row of plane trees edged the driveway, and silhouetted against the sky as one looked toward the street were two very tall ginkgo trees. There were big yew bushes, masses of blue lace-cap hydrangea and pachysandra growing under all the trees, and huge *Rhododendron maximum* plants along the street. Finally, I was completely fascinated by the old basement and the possibilities it offered.

Here was my first chance to start from scratch on landscape, architecture, and interiors all combined, and with myself as client! It took a lot of letters back and forth to finally get the thing settled; I took possession of the property in the fall of 1965. I knew it would be a while before I could design the house, find a contractor, and get it built, so I rented a small apartment right in the center of the village, which I could use as a base of operations during the construction period.

The first thing I did was to buy a collection of garden tools and start clearing the property of all the dead cedar trees, vines, and debris. Truckloads of trash went to the dump. I removed a brick walkway with a bordering hedge of Japanese yew which bisected the front yard, as I did not want an entrance into the center of the property and I knew everyone would come by car and enter from the driveway. I took out a row of althaea bushes (rose of Sharon) on either side of the yew hedges because these are my least favorite plants. They try unsuccessfully to look like hibiscus, which I love, and they are always covered with ants.

To ensure the privacy I treasure, I put up a high cedar fence across the street side of the property and all along the driveway. There was already a high open wood fence on part of the boundary at the back, and I extended this all the way across. This left open only the east side of the property, facing the converted theatre, but there a

Above The original building on the property, a shingle-style summer house built around the turn of the century. *Right* The new house.

group of Austrian pines, rhododendron, other shrubs, and some mounds of vines all blocked the view.

I wanted the house to be a simple garden shelter, tied into the existing elements of garden by fingers of deck extending out in different directions and down into the sunken area. I hate "foundation" plantings and feel that a house should stand apart from its garden but yet be tied to it in different ways. I wanted to create as much variety as possible within the acre, with different places to walk, sit or lie in the sun, look at the sky, or listen to the birds. The decks would tie the whole thing together and separate the house from the garden at the same time. I also wanted to make dramatic use of the basement and the possibilities it offered for growing delicate plants in a protected climate. I wanted some of the things I loved in Alabama gardens—*Magnolia grandiflora, banksia* roses, and scuppernong vines. And I had them all.

I was fortunate to again have Earl Pope's help with structural and detail drawings. We agreed that the house should rise out of the basement from the base of the T, facing north. This would provide a sunny southern exposure with views over the garden for the main living spaces. Small and symmetrical in plan, which emphasized the asymmetry of the surrounding open spaces and decks, the house was truly a garden shelter. It has been described in many different ways by many different visitors. The harpsichordist Albert Fuller described it as "Versailles comes to Kyoto," and gave it the name Serene Surroundings. Aaron Copland said it was the perfect place to write music. To the casual visitor the house, with its open-plan living-dining space, post-and-beam construction in natural wood contrasting with white walls, matchstick bamboo roll-up blinds, and simple floor lamps with large white paper globes for shades (which I had designed), seemed "Japanese." But the house was Oriental only in essence and not in detail.

I dislike the inhuman scale of high cathedral-like ceilings, preferring instead construction that extends one's vision in horizontal directions to include sky, trees, and garden. The central section of the house had continuous floor-to-ceiling narrow panels of glass, some of which were doors opening onto the decks. Later I added several small square windows in the sitting area so that the panoramic view of the garden continued as you passed through the space.

I tried out different arrangements of furniture and art in the main living-dining space, with the idea of changing schemes to fit the

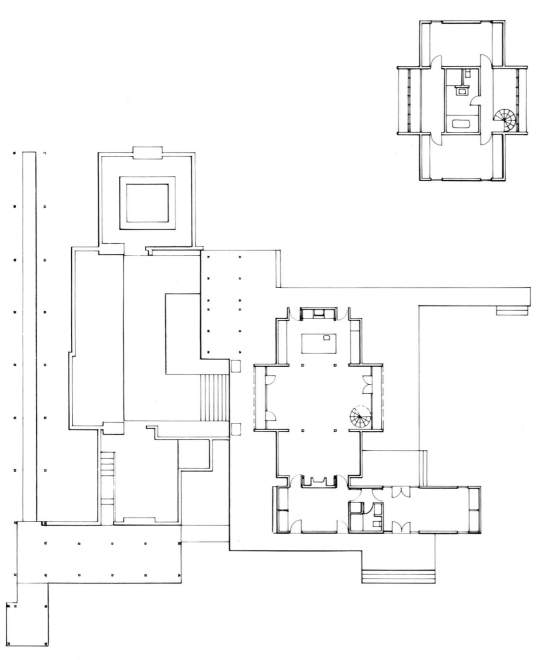

Above Plan of house. Both floors were originally symmetrical until addition of workroom and guest room. *Far right* South side of the house overlooking the sunken garden. *Near right* The same view several years later.

Central living-dining area. The big
five-by-ten-foot table served as both
dining and work/study table. The
white metal spiral stair provides
access to the upper floor.

seasons. A garden is never static—shapes, textures, and colors change—and I think a house should be the same. The furnishings were not important in themselves. No rare antiques or collections of bibelots. I built a big five-by-ten-foot table out of fir plywood (like that used for Ping-Pong tables) and six-by-six wood legs, and this served as my library/dining table. The top was waxed and left natural, and there was room on the top for flowers, books, and a Luxo lamp for reading. The chairs were comfortable Loom armchairs painted black (mass produced, these were used mostly as porch furniture).

In the "living" end of the space were several platforms built of plywood and covered in charcoal indoor-outdoor carpet which were used in a variety of ways. There were also a few moveable chairs and a settee of my own design (from my collection for Jack Lenor Larsen). Two bronze floor lamps designed by Alberto Giacometti, which I had bought from him in Paris many years ago, fit perfectly into the scheme.

Upstairs was a large sky-lit bathroom, situated in the center with identical bedrooms at each end. I used one of these as my room, my bed being the big four-poster mahogany bed from Kintray. A few years later I added a wing to the house with a workroom, bath, and guest room, which opened out into the garden on two sides.

The East Hampton place had everything I value in a house—privacy, simple spaces full of light with openings on all sides into a garden, easy maintenance (there were slate floors downstairs and solid blue linoleum from Holland upstairs), a comfortable place to prepare food, and a beautiful room to bathe in. And finally, it was uncluttered with things that have to be dusted and protected.

To me successful houses are those where you feel a strong sense of the people living in them, people who do what is natural to them and don't give a damn for the fashion of the moment. The houses of artists like Alexander Calder, Saul Steinberg, and Tino Nivola all give you an immediate feeling of the joy of living and the life that breathes in the house.

I once visited the Sarabhai house in India designed by Le Corbusier. I had never met the owners, and they were traveling in Europe at the time, but I have never been anywhere where I felt so strongly the personalities of the people who lived in a place. The mixture of beautiful old Indian chests and textiles with contemporary chairs by Charles Eames and the simple spaces in concrete opening to the outside all made a strong personal statement. In one room, along

Left Kitchen area. Freestanding work counter houses hi-fi speakers and storage for vases; floor-to-ceiling storage cabinets along two walls. *Below* View from living area toward kitchen.

with some rare old textiles, they had torn out magazine reproductions of paintings they loved and thumbtacked them to the walls. This takes real know-how, but too many people are afraid to make a personal statement—to express what they are in their houses. Instead they end up living in cold mausoleums—monuments to their architects. The architectural shell is important but only as a jumping-off place. The life of a house starts after that.

It is unusual to have a garden dictate the design of the house, but that's what happened in my case. My garden developed step-by-step over a period of twenty years. The only successful way to make a personal garden is by trial and error. If you try something and then discover after a time that it's not right, be ruthless. Yank it out. The first rule is learning to say "no" to friends who offer you plants you don't really want. Of course, some offers are gratefully received if the material fits into what you are trying to achieve. In this day, when every little plant costs ten times what it did a short time ago, one is delighted when a gardening friend decides to divide the Japanese iris or the Hyperion daylilies and offers you as many as you can cart away. Sharing with other gardeners is a special joy—one loves the plants all the more because they came from a friend's garden.

Very early on I discovered that all of the beautiful pictures in magazines and books of the great gardens of England, France, and Italy are very misleading. The photographs are taken when everything is at its very peak of full bloom. Nobody tells you that should there be a battering rain or a sudden drop in temperature the next day the owner would be forced to say, "You should have seen it last week." So it is important to give the garden an architectural skeleton and enough permanent planting so it will hold its own no matter what disasters come along. Being an architect, this is my natural tendency anyway.

In the case of my East Hampton home, the old basement was already a big asset. It consisted of three spaces—a large central area with small "rooms" at both ends. I built a wide flight of steps going down from the deck into the center of the large space below, leaving room for plants on both sides. I put in three dwarf apple trees on one side with ferns as groundcover and two *Magnolia virginianas* on the side toward the house and trained climbing hydrangea and *banksia* rose on the brick walls. On the deck above this area I built an arbor and covered it with scuppernong vines and white wisteria that grew up from the planting area below. This arbor had a table and benches

Facing page The sitting area, showing different furniture arrangements. *Top left* Platforms pushed together as a place to lounge in front of the fire in chilly weather; a pair of eighteenth-century Japanese screens with flowers on gold paper occupy the niches. *Top right* Platforms removed; seating group consisting of chairs of my own design, including Warwick chair, Bub chair and sofa. *Bottom* Platforms for art and seat cushions in niches; high-back folding chairs in black leather; cowhides on the slate floor. *Above* Looking into the wild garden through the narrow panels of glass on the north side.

Upper hallway with bathroom on right and master bedroom beyond. Ceilings are natural cedar flooring.

and was a pleasant place to have lunch in the shadow of the vines.

In one of the smaller rooms, I left the old concrete floor and built a raised square pool. I tried growing lotus and water lilies, but the bugs were too much for me and I gave it up. The walls of this room were completely covered with Boston ivy, the leaves like bright green overlapping feathers. Just above the pool, on the upper level, I made my sculpture *Homage to Luis Barragán.* Inspired by a window in Barragán's house in Mexico, it was a simple cross in a wood frame supported at the bottom by an opening in the brick wall which had been a window. Barragán was pleased with *Homage* and said it should be painted Day-Glo red; he even sent me a color sample. So Day-Glo red it was—beautiful against all the surrounding greens.

In the room at the other end of the basement, I bricked the floor over the old concrete and put in a narrow brick stair going to the upper level. The existing Lally column that supported a beam of the old house was used as a base for a bronze lotus sculpture with a copper tendril twining down around the column. This was designed and made by Marcia Weese, a Chicago sculptor. She also made an abstract sculpture called *House* in Corten steel and copper, which I placed on one of the old chimney foundations; it provided an important accent in the view from the living room windows.

The next step was to build an L-shaped wooden arbor running the entire length of the basement at the upper level, which lifted the eye out of the sunken garden to the plantings above and provided shade over a brick walk leading into the garden from the driveway. At the end of the long side of the arbor I built a screened gazebo, which was a favorite place to have lunch or a late afternoon drink during the buggy season. At the east end of the house I put a raised rose garden in which was a twisted column in sand-blasted stainless steel made by the Mexican sculptor Ricardo Reggazzoni, who lives in New York. On an axis with a glass door opening from the workroom, this sculpture was also visible from the living area.

The area on the north side of the house was made into a wild garden, with masses of oak-leaf hydrangea and *superbum* lilies growing under the renovated arbor on the original concrete pillars. This was covered with pink *Clematis montana,* spectacular in May. I kept the original plane trees around the driveway on the west side of the property. They made a circle around a huge dogwood tree underplanted with pachysandra. Behind this circle, on the blank wall of the garage, I put espaliered pears.

Top left My bedroom. The big four-poster bed was made around 1850 in Mobile, Alabama, and has solid mahogany posts; the bedcover is an old family quilt; a maple chopping block forms the built-in shelf. *Bottom left* The ground-floor guest room opens into the garden on two sides. I designed the half-round light fixtures with pleated Swiss cotton shades. *Below* The sky-lit bathroom.

The platforms from the living area pushed together in front of the window overlooking the sunken garden— a perfect spot for afternoon naps.

Once I was settled in the house in East Hampton I could turn my attention to finding a warm place to spend the cold months. My choice of the west coast of Florida as a place to make my winter headquarters was not arrived at overnight. I bought an inflatable plastic globe of the world and hung it near my desk. I looked at Morocco and remembered how cold I had been in the house on Anfa Hill in Casablanca during my Navy duty in 1942. The masses of magenta bougainvillea spilling over the roof and the heavy branches of yellow acacia brushing against the house had not compensated for the icy tile floors and the dampness from those thick stuccoed walls. I daydreamed about Tunisia—the wild anemones, the screaming peacocks, and the beautiful white-domed houses looking out over the sea. This, however, reminded me of Greece and the Easter I'd spent there shivering in a heavy sweater and jacket. Portugal seemed possible for a while after a friend told me about a ruin he'd bought for a song and remodeled into a charming compound of stone structures around a walled garden. But I checked the international weather reports in the *New York Times* and found that the area near Lisbon has about the same winter temperature as New York City, with more dampness.

All of these places seemed so far away, and I knew I wanted to have easy access to New York. Furthermore, they were expensive to get to easily, and I had started out with the idea that I wanted to be where friends could visit me at modest transportation cost. For a while the Caribbean seemed like a possibility. After making a number of trips there over a period of several years, in 1969 I bought property near the town of Phillipsburg on the Dutch side of St. Maarten in the Dutch Antilles. But life in the islands seemed to be more and more uncertain. Although it has some of the most beautiful beaches I know of, St. Maarten is dry and barren and water is a serious problem—a big limitation on gardening. Since there is no commercial gardening, food is mostly imported. It is even difficult to get fresh fish since the natives avoid it, believing it to be poisoned by something in the reefs. And then there is the problem of getting back and forth. The winter is, of course, the busy season there, and the planes are jammed with tourists.

Finally, I looked at the plant zone map and found that the most tropical area in the States starts around Sarasota in south Florida, meaning that the warm-weather plants I love could be grown there. I associated Sarasota with the circus, because I knew it had been their winter headquarters, and I knew about the Ringling Museum and art school. I had also seen pictures of houses by Paul Rudolph, designed when he was working in Sarasota with Ralph Twitchell, as well as of the buildings I. M. Pei had designed for the New College of the University of South Florida. So I set off for Sarasota knowing the name of one local architect and with a strong desire to explore the area.

I spent a few days just looking around, then drove on to Key West, stopping to visit Corkscrew Swamp, the Everglades, and various nurseries along the roads. I found the countryside, wherever it was still in a natural state, to be wonderful. Then I went back to Sarasota, rented a place for a few weeks, and continued my research. I discovered that there are two beaches: the one called Lido is composed mostly of crushed shells and is not very long; the other, Siesta Beach, has soft white sand which packs hard along the water where it is wet. This beach, a long, flat curve—about an hour's walk from one end to the other and back again—was perfect for my daily hike. Having decided I would like to find a place within short driving distance of this beach, I made a list of my other requirements:

- privacy, or the possibility of creating it
- orientation with the back of the house toward the south
- water of some kind on at least one side of the property
- a lot size scaled to the amount of gardening I could handle myself
- a one-story structure with a simple shape in not too good a condition

I knew I would want to rip out most of the insides of any house, but I wanted to end up with two or three bedrooms, a good-size kitchen, living and dining space, and a pleasant place for working.

So I fanned out in different directions from my chosen beach and drove up and down streets looking at places with "For Sale" signs, jotting down addresses and always making notes on plants I liked that seemed to be doing well in the local environment. It wasn't until the following year that I found the house on Flamingo Avenue. A real-estate agent who had seemed sympathetic and understanding as I described in detail what I was trying to find showed it to me. She was apologetic, assuring me that, while it was somewhat of a disaster area, down underneath it did meet some of my requirements.

My first visit was completely depressing—a run-down yard with one tree (*Albizia lebbek*, or woman's tongue) and a low hedge of Brazilian pepper along one street, glitter-covered concrete blocks, windows that were too high, bright blue trim, and an unpleasant

Flamingo Avenue, Sarasota

Back of the Sarasota house reflected in the lagoon (after the second remodeling).

smell. Inside, after a narrow entrance passage with plastic vines in planters, was a living room with a pool table and dirty shag carpet, a cathedral ceiling that was much too high and out of scale with the space, and a fireplace that was a designer's nightmare. Made of brick, stone, and concrete block, it had "Chinese" bookshelves and a raised hearth that extended out into the room in a long zucchini shape at the end of which was a metal column supporting the ridge of the roof. The kitchen was all in bright, shiny green with another high metal window above the sink counter. Beyond the end of the living room was a porch, obviously added, with aluminum awning windows on three sides, walls of imitation wood paneling, and a sloping ceiling covered with acoustical tiles embedded with sparkles. To the left of the entrance were three bedrooms and two baths. One bedroom had black wallpaper with flowers, and its bathroom had a corner shower I could barely get into.

I had to come back several times before I could look beyond all of this and concentrate on the potential of the place. The neighborhood was good, and it was convenient to town and my beach. There was a shopping center a few blocks away. It was on a corner with a hedge already planted on the long side (only later did I discover why hedges of Brazilian pepper were so unpopular with local homeowners. Birds like the bright red berries and the seeds they drop come up everywhere; the plant grows overnight and can really get out of hand). Perhaps the greatest asset was the little lagoon behind the house on the south side. It was enclosed all around by a border of mangrove with its shiny leaves and hanging bomb-shaped seeds, making it seem like my own private pond. I could see only the boat dock of the house on the other side and part of the roof of a house above the trees. I later learned that the lagoon opened into the bay through a narrow passage deep enough for a good-size boat to go through.

The lot was just big enough, with a narrow strip of ground along the house on the east and a wide strip on the west, in which, toward the back of the house, stood the single tree. I could already imagine a fence and arbors with vines and lots of bamboo. There was one house opposite mine, but it was behind a hedge of hibiscus, oleander, and sea grape and there were large oak trees all around it. So my problem on that side would be only to screen out people on the street, and I already had the hedge as a starter. The garage faced west on the long side of the property. I saw immediately that by shifting the garage opening to the north end I could make a larger park-

ing area and be able to extend the garden strip all the way along the west side.

I was hooked. Next time I came with a folding rule and a pad of paper and took all the measurements so I could make a drawing of the house and yard. Then I told the agent I would buy it. While the papers were being drawn up, I asked several local architects about contractors they would recommend and managed to find a very agreeable one who proved to be excellent. He did all of the carpentry, with two helpers, and arranged for sub-contractors to do the plumbing, heating and air conditioning, electrical work, and such. I rented a room with a terrace in a friend's house a few blocks away, where I set up a drafting table. During the day I worked at the site because of the need to constantly check measurements. By the time the house was officially mine, I had the plan and elevations finished and had started work on the details. The remodeling took five weeks. I was there a great deal of the time, working out details with the carpenters, shopping for hardware and light fixtures, and trying to keep a step ahead with my drawings.

We practically gutted the place. The smallest bedroom, to the left of the front door, was completely demolished to provide a spacious entrance hall with a big storage closet for the washer-dryer units and cleaning equipment. A sort of utility room behind this was also torn out to become the new kitchen. The entrance hall opened directly into the kitchen without any door, but the view of the kitchen work area was blocked by creating a double back-to-back niche enclosing the refrigerator on the kitchen side and a shelf with recessed lighting above it on the hall side. This element was freestanding, a narrow slot having been left between it and the edge of the long counter-top with sink, stove, and cabinets, which runs the entire length of the adjacent wall. Opposite the counter and parallel to it we built a long, low narrow unit with shelves. The solid back of this unit faces toward the dining area and blocks the view of the kitchen work top when you are seated at the dining table.

The basic shape and size of the living-dining area remained the same. The house already occupied the maximum area permitted by the set-back requirements of the local building code, so it could not be extended on any side. However, the relocation of the kitchen provided a spacious area for dining directly behind the fireplace, so that the living-dining area now made a U-shaped space around the fireplace. The raised hearth was removed, the whole fireplace element

Left The original fireplace unit with its hodge-podge of materials. *Below* Plan of remodeled spaces.

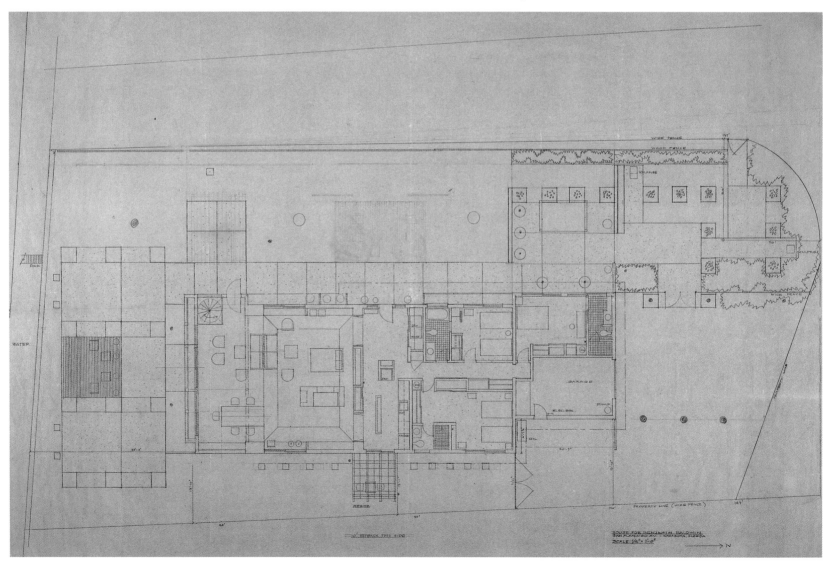

was lowered and separated from the wall on the kitchen side, and the bookcases were removed. I did keep a niche in the end of the fireplace which had been some sort of grill. I use this for displaying a very beautiful old bowl from Santo Domingo.

The ceiling was changed to a tray ceiling, the scale of which seemed perfect for the room. The walls were built out to create niches for shelves, a long banquette seat in the dining area, and a platform for cushions along the wall next to the porch. All of the existing windows were removed and large sliding doors were installed. In the porch I left the windows on the south, facing the lagoon, but removed those on the two end walls and made these walls solid, with a door in one leading outside to the garden. All of the paneling and acoustical tile was re-moved and replaced with sheetrock, which was used throughout the house. I added two four-foot-square skylights, which open for ventila-tion, and built a platform seat directly behind the one in the living room.

The floors throughout the house were terrazzo, which I left but later covered with indoor-outdoor charcoal grey carpet—the terrazzo was cold to bare feet. I put the same carpeting over the two long seat-ing platforms as well as a large freestanding platform in front of the fireplace. The dark grey color is very handsome with the white walls, makes a quiet background for a number of kilim rugs I have collected over the years, and ties the whole interior space together in a unified whole. I wanted a hard tight feeling underfoot, as far removed as pos-sible from the repulsive shag carpet so favored in Florida.

The bedrooms got sliding glass doors also and large areas of storage with sliding louvered doors stained brown-black. The bath with the corner shower was enlarged considerably to include a spacious tiled shower. Each of these rooms now looks out into parts of the garden.

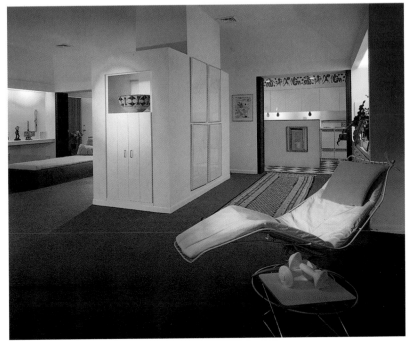

After I lived in the house a few years, I did a second remodeling, making half of the garage into a second guest bedroom and bath. I also took out the porch and made that space part of the living-dining area. Above this I added a second-floor workroom, reached by a spiral stair, and did a new arbor at the side toward the street. This was a great improvement because it both gave me a large workroom sep-arate from the ground-floor living space and provided a larger area for dining as well as space for a second seating group. New sliding doors all across the back of the house provided much more light and air and a beautiful outlook over the lagoon.

Making the garden in Sarasota was a delight. I was already familiar with a great deal of tropical plant material from my trips to St.

Below The living-dining space after my final remodeling, view toward fireplace with platform in front. African dance mask from Ghana on fireplace wall; crocodile boat from New Guinea above.

Maarten and the Caribbean islands, but there was a lot to learn. Everywhere I went I looked at the things growing and doing well and found out the names of the plants I liked. I went to dozens of nurseries and spent many happy hours walking around looking and making notes. I went to all the bookstores and gradually got together a sizeable collection of books on gardening in the tropics and various types of plants. I wanted to limit myself to things that would be happy in my particular location and to have a lot of a few things rather than a little of everything in the books.

I love arbors and vines so I started with those. By putting up a cypress fence along the outer edge of my long planting strip on the street side and building an arbor at each end, I was able to create a nice play of spaces along the side of the house. I paved the areas under these arbors and the connecting strip between them with concrete (with the aggregate exposed) divided into sections by a wooden framework of two-by-fours. Partly covered by the overhang of the roof, the connecting strip provided a walk along the house.

It was easy to pick a vine for the arbors. My favorite of all vines is *Thunbergia grandiflora*. Years ago I had cut out a picture of a thunbergia vine growing over a bamboo trellis in Hawaii, with long racemes of white flowers hanging down to the ground. It was love at first sight. I knew from my reference books that it would grow in Sarasota, but I could find only blue varieties growing in the gardens around town. So I used that for the time being. But it was such a rampant grower that, when I remodeled the arbor, I replaced it with Confederate jasmine.

In my enthusiasm to minimize maintenance, I decided to eliminate all of the grass—against the advice of two neighbors who had been in residence for some years. Since I planned to make most of the space on the north side of the house into a parking area and the entire strip along the west of the house was to be arbors and planting, the only areas left with grass were the narrow piece along the east and the part to the south of the house by the lagoon. I had two men come with a huge machine that scooped up the sod, going down several inches. After leveling the area, they sprayed it all with weed-killer and covered it entirely with black vinyl, over which they spread several inches of small grey stones. They assured me that I would not have a weed for at least three years. That was just the challenge the nut grass needed. It promptly revved up production and was popping through the stones in less than a month. After a year of trying to keep this under control with various weed-killing sprays, I made life simpler by

Left Front entrance showing garden outside. *Below* Kitchen with frieze under Plexiglas of a print by Matisse; under the counter is a plugmold strip with incandescent bulbs with green metal shades.

Below The seating group facing the
water with spiral stair going to upstairs workroom.

Top Detail of the tray ceiling in the dining area. *Bottom* View of living-dining space looking toward the water (every room in the house opens into the surrounding garden).

paving most of the south area as well as the section at the entrance from the parking area. Again I used concrete with exposed aggregate, divided into sections by wood strips.

Before doing this, however, I had built another wood deck, out close to the water. This was attached to four large cypress planters, which were part of a group of twelve laid on the stones in rows. I visualized this area as a kind of orangerie and planted calamondin oranges in the twelve planters, with dwarf Confederate jasmine hanging down around the sides. But various windstorms, including one of hurricane proportions named Agnes, made the calamondins look very unhappy in their boxes, so I finally went out of the citrus business and gave them all to a friend. They were followed by *Philodendron selloum,* which seemed to like the set-up better. I have since changed this to Texas sage with a border of dwarf jasmine.

When the area by the lagoon was paved, I left a wide planting bed along each side and also directly in front of the house itself. My thought was to make this area as green and jungly as possible, and I put in a number of *Ficus benjamina* (weeping fig), Gatlea guavas, and philodendron. The bed along the house is stuffed full of dwarf bamboo and marguerites, with Confederate jasmine vines growing up at both ends and across the edge of the roof overhang. I also transplanted two mango trees to this bed with the thought that it would be good to have some shade over the porch, which I used as a workroom, and over the deck by the water.

My two favorite plants are bamboo and lotus, both greatly loved by designers of ancient gardens in China. Since I have planted my gardens in Sarasota and East Hampton I have discovered that many of the trees and plants I love most were favorites in Chinese gardens—pine trees, bamboo, peonies, lotus, chrysanthemum, persimmon, poppies, lilies, hibiscus, daylilies, iris, hosta, and the gingko tree. In Chinese lore, bamboo was the symbol of pliability and strength, of hardy age and long friendship. Like a gentleman, it bows to the storm but rises again and always remains green. The chrysanthemum was the symbol of long life, the flower of retirement and culture. The king of flowers, peony was the symbol of material prosperity, of wealth and happiness. And the lotus was the symbol of purity and truth, of noble endeavor. It grows up spotless out of the mud (material world) through the water (emotional middle region) to the surface and free air (world of the spirit). It is the unfolding and flowering of the human spirit.

Palma Terrace, East Hampton

I decided to feature bamboo in the planting bed to the west of the house. I now have four different kinds growing there, including the giant bamboo that is so beautiful in Japanese forests. This is just outside my bedroom, and I love watching it blow in the wind and hearing the strange music it makes when one stem rubs against another one. I don't know of any plant more beautiful—the segmented design, the extraordinary color of fresh green, the shape of the leaves and the way they come out of the main stalk, even the dead leaves covering the ground underneath.

My dream house in Florida would have a big pool full of pink Egyptian lotus, an arbor covered with *Thunbergia grandiflora* enclosing a courtyard with pots of hibiscus—all set in a grove of giant bamboo. A cardboard model of just such a place hangs near my work table.

In the spring of 1988 I had open heart surgery in Sarasota, and when I went back to East Hampton, I soon realized that I could no longer cope with so much house and garden. It was getting more difficult to find any experienced help and maintenance of the place was too much for my declining energy. So I decided it was time to move on to something smaller, scaled to what I thought I could manage.

It was not easy for me to give up the beautiful garden I had worked twenty years to create. It is a simple matter to reproduce a house from drawings, but never a garden. It grows from love and returns that love many times over. It was a sad day for me when I locked the house and drove out of the driveway for the last time.

I had, however, found a smaller house and looked forward to a new challenge. And a challenge it was. I liked the location; it was within walking distance of the village in an area that had been a nursery, so there were lovely specimens of both weeping and cut-leaf beech and a lot of deciduous flowering trees. At the edge of the driveway was a beautiful beech and on the other side of the front yard an enormous flowering crabapple. The trees around the perimeter of the backyard were dead or dying and vines had taken over. The first priority was to clear the debris and put up a high fence around three sides of the property. I wanted the garden to be completely closed in and have the private feeling of a monastery garden.

I made measured drawings of the house and found a contractor who could work on the remodeling over the winter, while I was in Florida. The shell of the house was fine and the roof was new but the inside was terrible, so once again I gutted the whole thing. An L-

Above A corner of the living area.
Right Various views of the living area.

Above View from the porch into the garden; the stainless steel sculpture is by Ricardo Reggazzoni. *Top right* Details. *Bottom right* The porch.

shaped entrance hall ran around the living room with two bathrooms opening into it. I took all of this out, which made the living space much larger, and put in a freestanding storage cabinet, creating a protected entry at the front door. The cabinet could be opened from both sides and at the top and provided storage for coats and work materials as well as having a niche in the center for a piece of sculpture.

The master bedroom, which opened into the back garden, was enlarged and space taken out of the front guest room to create a walk-in closet for the bigger room and a new bath for the guest room. By closing up the bathroom doors, I was able to create a long niche with a display shelf, storage cabinets below, and recessed lighting.

I plastered over the fireplace bricks and raised the opening off the floor. I added bookshelves with storage cabinets below to the spaces on each side of the projecting fireplace and a tall cabinet for television and hi-fi. By removing a small bedroom on the garden side, I opened up the living space to the garden, making the space L-shaped. All of the windows were replaced with larger ones, those facing the back garden with sliding glass doors opening onto a deck.

The kitchen was completely redone with all new equipment. One good feature was a roofed porch at the back. I raised the floor from ground to kitchen level, screened the whole thing, and made a redwood deck which I extended across the entire back of the house. This had full-width wood steps down the garden.

I wanted this garden to have an architectural feeling, which I tried to achieve through a combination of structural elements (arches), planters, a trellis, sculpture, and shrubs pruned as standards and hedges, as well as the arrangement of plants in large clumps. Thus the shapes of plants and plantings were used to extend the sense of architecture from inside to outside.

There are twenty-five arches in all, a row of five on the axis of the sliding doors to the master bedroom and the living room, two rows around the herb garden, centered on the screened porch off the kitchen, and the others around the central "cloister" section, which has a fountain with wood planter boxes around it. The arches are in a double row behind this section and are covered with New Dawn roses. All the others have spring- and fall-blooming clematis. Completing the enclosure of the central section is a six-foot-high hedge of *Rhamnus* (Tallhedge) underplanted in *Nepeta.* Around the entire perimeter is a curving bed of shrubs, small trees, and perennials. The green lawn ties the whole scheme together.

Non-Residential Spaces

The following section shows that my design principles (as outlined in the previous chapter) remain the same when applied to non-residential spaces.

Executive Offices, Solo Cup Company, Chicago

Clockwise from left Fin walls in offices.
Cup we designed. In the glass-front
cases are examples of Solo's line of
cups.

Cosco Showroom, Chicago

In 1959 I designed the executive offices for the Solo Cup Company, dividing the spaces in the executive offices with fin walls which do not reach the ceiling. I did some research on drinking cups through the ages, and used photographs of these mounted on panels in various areas.

About the same time, Clarence Hamilton asked me to design the showroom for kitchen furniture made by the Hamilton Manufacturing Corporation (Cosco). They had taken space at the Chicago Furniture Mart and wanted to do a simple, low-budget display.

Top I did the whole corridor wall in glass, stenciled their trade name above this in several colors, and lighted this upper area with a row of exposed bulbs. *Bottom* The interior space was divided by semi-transparent white matchstick blinds and lamps with Swedish paper shades were hung above tables and the reception desk.

Ritz Bar, Boston

In 1968 the Ritz Hotel asked me to give The Bar a new look, so I ripped out the dowdy fake French interior and took down the heavy drapes from the windows looking out on Boston Commons to let in daylight. I divided the space into two levels with a central bar located opposite the entrance.

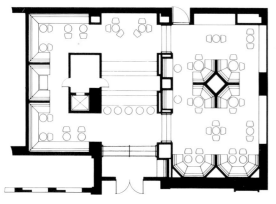

Above The walls of the central bar area were done in English walnut and the other walls in padded fabric panels to minimize noise. *Left* The hanging sculpture in Plexiglas was made by Sydney Butchkes. *Far left* Plan of the redesigned space.

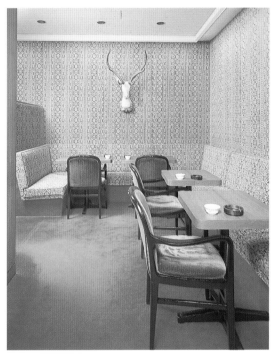

Above An all-over gros-point pattern covers walls on the upper level as well as some of the chairs which I designed especially for this job (This "Ritz" chair later was included in my furniture collection for Jack Lenor Larsen). *Left* The niches and channeled banquettes on the lower, "street," level are upholstered in olive green velour. The gilded wall sconces came from the old Ritz Hotel in New York.

Phillips Exeter, Library and Dining Hall, New Hampshire

Louis Kahn asked me to do the furnishings for the library and dining hall he was building for Phillips Exeter Academy. The furnishings had to be very simple, not competitive with the architecture, and built to withstand the beating of slouching students. Kahn wanted to hang banners from the high ceiling in the dining hall so we did about fifty designs for his approval. While he was looking at them he did some rough sketches of his own ideas after which he dashed off to catch a train to Philadelphia. The young architect who was representing Lou at the job in Exeter stayed on, and I commented to him that I didn't think there was enough information to have the sketches executed. "Oh," he said, "we've done whole buildings from less than that!"

Left The library. *Above* The Elm Street dining hall.

Yale Center for British Art, New Haven

I worked on the last building done by Louis Kahn—the Yale Center for British Art donated to Yale University by Paul Mellon. Lou died before the building was finished, but he had told the people at Yale he would like me to work on the furnishings. Anthony Pellecchia and Marshall Meyers, who took over the completion of the museum, asked me to continue with them. Jules Proun and Bob Kuehn were representing the university for the job and Kingman Brewster, president of Yale at that time, kept an eye on progress. The director of the museum, Edmund Pillsbury, acted as our contact with Mr. Mellon, who showed keen interest in every detail. I have never worked with a more cooperative group.

Right In the Library Court English oak panels fill the spaces between the structural elements. The concrete well for the elevator and circular stair was left exposed. The only furnishings are four oversized tufted couches in dark leather and a long wall table for flowers. *Far right* In the library we used the same trestle tables and chairs that Lou had liked in the Phillips Exeter dining hall, along with groups of comfortable upholstered armchairs.

Gallery space with Chadwick seating.

Katcher Banks, Miami

Since I have been spending winters in Florida, I have worked on a number of jobs for Gerald Katcher besides his house in Coconut Grove. These include two banks and offices for Mr. Katcher's law firm. In the banks I used light woods in conjunction with simply framed prints and photographs to create cheerful, pleasant places to work.

Branch office.

Clockwise from top Chairman's office.
Reception area for executive offices.
Customer service area.

Clockwise from top left Executive office.
Executive office. Customer service area.

Americana Hotel, Fort Worth

In 1980 I was asked by Sid Bass to design the interiors for the Americana Hotel he was building in Fort Worth, Texas. I was pleased to have this opportunity to do designs for another hotel and took the job, working with my assistant Jonathan Warwick and associate designer Roger Ferri. To me a hotel should not try to be Disneyland but rather a home away from home—a quiet, restful place to relax in a serene atmosphere after a busy day of business and social activities, meetings, and sight-seeing. I look for space that is human in scale, not overpowering; for richness and elegance in materials and colors; for simplicity and comfort in furnishings. This was our approach in designing the interiors of the Americana.

Left The reception desk, in English brown oak, underneath a cantilevered balcony from which water drips into the two reflecting pools below. *Top right* Kitty Weese, myself, and Harry Weese at the opening day party at the Americana. *Right center and bottom* Around the pools are groups of comfortable upholstered seating.

The ballroom was designed to provide a low-key background for the varied activities it accommodates. The treatment of the wall panels and ceiling sets up a rhythm that is pleasing to the eye; the muted colors work well as a background for both fanciful parties and commercial displays. The moveable wall panels and changeable lighting make the room highly versatile.

Left The ballroom at night.
Above The entrance to the ballroom.

Above A muted color scheme similar
to that in the lobby was used in the
cocktail lounge. Seating is provided
by my pivoting upholstered Bub
chairs from the Larsen collection.
Right View of the cocktail lounge on
the cantilevered balcony.

The concept of simple elegance was carried through all the details from table settings for food service to furnishings, carpets, and fabrics throughout the hotel. Every comfort is provided in the rooms and suites. Materials and colors are practical and cheerful. A special point of interest was the selection of art for the guest rooms. All of the pictures on the walls are custom reproductions of works of art in the various museums of Fort Worth, so one can choose between Matisse and Remington. The selection was made by Mrs. Richard Brown, whose husband was curator of the Kimbell Museum in Fort Worth until his death. I hope we created interiors which impress not by jarring the senses and confusing the eye but by providing the traveler with a relaxing and gracious environment in which he would not regret spending some days of his life.

Left In the gourmet restaurant, Reflections, I used my Ritz armchairs at tables arranged on several levels around a central shallow pool, out of which rise three plant-like columns topped by abstract lotus flowers. The ceiling was painted dark blue behind the white plastic lattice. *Top right* Guest bedrooms have comfortable lounge seating around tables for writing or dining. Color schemes vary on different floors. *Bottom right* Another cocktail area with Warwick chairs.

Details

There are certain details that occur over and over in the jobs I have done for myself and for my clients and these have become typical of my design work. The illustrations that follow present a selection of these details and identify the jobs from which they are taken. All of these projects have been published in magazines or books (see Bibliography, page 198).

Large-scale Built-in Seating

The front hall at Kintray, our family's country house in Alabama. The built-in seat under the bookcases opposite the big fireplace is where it all started. The chrome yellow English bowl on the table held pear blossoms in the spring and masses of goldenrod and grasses in the fall. The low Mexican chair in woven webbing is also chrome yellow. The pillow covers with shaggy stripes were woven by me on my Cranbrook loom and the vase on the shelf above was made by Maija Grotell.

A simple weekend house which I built for a cousin, Alice Pye, on a lake near Montgomery, Alabama. The built-in seat provides extra sleeping places. The other furniture is Aalto and Mathsson from my sister Kitty's shop, Baldwin Kingrey, in Chicago.

A slightly more sophisticated vacation house near Fort Walton, Florida. The long bench seating reduces the need for pull-up chairs and enlarges the feeling of space. The chairs from Knoll are covered in the Baldwin-Machado printed fabric called "Barrel Heads."

Living room in a Chicago professor's house. A built-in platform across one entire side of the room provides both seating in the deep recess with its shuttered windows and display space for pictures and art objects. The oval red lacquered table is Korean and the lamp is by Isamu Noguchi. The antique deck chairs have sheepskin throws.

A house designed by Fred Mertz for a lawyer in Brooklyn Heights, New York. A built-in platform with comfortable cushions across one end of the seating area emphasizes the simple details of the architecture and enlarges the feeling of space.

An architect's apartment in Chicago overlooking Lake Michigan. A built-in platform seat joins thick cantilevered granite shelves in forming a U around the living room and tying the whole space together. A comfortable sofa and three bergères in olive green velvet complete the scheme. The side walls are covered in natural linen panels, with a Conrad Marca-Relli collage near the fireplace. A black cowskin rug on the dark granite floor ties together the freestanding seating group. White matchstick blinds at the windows are lit from behind to give a warm glow of light at night.

A house designed by Edward L. Barnes for a newspaperman and his dancer wife in Wayzata, Minnesota. An L-shaped furniture arrangement focuses attention on the fireplace. Seat cushions with pillows and red fox throws raise the built-in platforms to a height comfortable for lounging and reading. The long Louis XIII leather sofa and the oversized cushions are in scale with the large size of the room.

A remodeled old Spanish-style house purchased by a lawyer in Coconut Grove, Florida. A full-width platform covered in blue tile makes the long, narrow room seem wider; on it are seat cushions (opposite one of the back-to-back sofas) as well as plants and other objects. The same blue tile is used in the recessed window seats.

Executive offices of the Tandy Corporation, overlooking Fort Worth, Texas. Instead of platforms, a U-shaped arrangement of oversized couches is used to tie the room together and focus attention on the executive desk.

The bi-level living room of a New York apartment overlooking Central Park. A low leather seat was used to mark the point where the floor drops down a step, allowing the elimination of an ugly iron railing and post.

Variety in Places to Eat

I think that eating should be a delightful
experience, done in a setting that is happy
and beautiful no matter how simple.

The Terrace Plaza Hotel in Cincinnati, Ohio, designed by Skidmore, Owings, and Merrill. *Far left and top left* The Gourmet Room, a round penthouse cantilevered over the side of the building, was the fancy place to dine in the hotel. Neutral furnishings were used to give full play to the bright spots of color in Joan Miró's mural. *Bottom left* The main dining room, which had a mural by Saul Steinberg, was on the eighth floor at the far end of the lobby. Here again the colors were kept neutral, but the room was bright and cheerful—a fun place to dine.

My house on North State Street in Chicago. *Above* The back room overlooking the garden doubled as first-floor guest quarters and informal dining area. *Right* Outside this room I built a wood deck leading into the simple garden with a central area of pea gravel divided by a shallow basin of water with a splashing jet, a happy place to have breakfast or lunch. At night tiny Italian light bulbs twinkled in the old mock orange tree with its fragrant white flowers. The tablecloth and dishes are Farnasetti designs from Milan.

Right A lakeshore apartment in Chicago. A table for two in the master bedroom provides the perfect place to have morning coffee while looking at Lake Michigan through flowering azaleas and primroses. The Fortuny fabric in yellow and natural on the wall panels was also used on the bedcover and pillows.

Left My house in Chicago. *Top* More formal dining was at the big oak table in the dining end of the living space. I like to use different chairs, china, and flowers for different occasions. Here the side chairs are by Mies van der Rohe and the scheme is blue and white; the dishes are decorated with Japanese carp. The deep greenhouse window looks out into the garden. *Bottom* Another dinner setting—this one for Valentine's Day. Cardboard squares in pink, red, and white cover the table top; the carnations are in the same colors. Pink conch shells and Venini obelisks add a festive touch. As an experiment I turned the magic squares painting by Paul Klee on its side.

Right Terrace joining a house and rose garden, both of which I designed, in Southampton, New York. The setting for lunch is under a big Italian market umbrella.

A south side Chicago house. *Above* In the formal dining area a large oval table stands under a chrome fixture which I designed for the room. The chairs and colored glass candle cups were made in Italy, as were the two Venini vases on the wall shelf, which was added to provide a place for serving buffet. *Right* Informal dining takes place in the kitchen, where the children usually have their meals at a round scrubbed oak table. The cut-out prints by Matisse, framed end to end, add color and fun. The plain gold paper screen hides a radiator.

126

Comfortable Seating for Conversation

One thing I have always insisted upon in my design work is that the result be comfortable. This is also true for the chairs and other seating I have designed over the years. If space permits, I like to provide more than one seating group, and if not, at least one conversation group that provides some chairs that are easily moved about. I dislike rigid arrangements and am forever trying new possibilities.

A house in Fort Worth, Texas, designed by I. M. Pei. The spaces in this house are large and varied enough to provide room for several different groups for conversation. My choice of colors, fabrics, and textures reflects an attempt to add a humanizing touch to the angular architecture. *Far left* The main entrance to the house is into a huge glass-covered atrium with a white marble floor, a fountain with plantings, a thirty-foot-high *Ficus* tree, and a one-piece glass window that looks out over the countryside. The owner likes to entertain and this space is used mostly for large dinner dances. (At one of these she made her entrance riding on an elephant.) The main seating areas are to the right of this large space and are wrapped around a large bar which can be opened up for entertaining. Here the ceilings had been lowered to a more human scale. I divided this space into three groups of furnishings. *Top left* The first group—a long sofa and comfortable pivoting armchairs—is all covered in bottle green velvet and arranged to focus on a terrace with a bronze *Horse and Rider* by Mariano Marini. For an adjacent area (not pictured) where paintings hung on fabric-covered walls, I designed a long, comfortable U-shaped seat with cushions in natural suede and added two custom-made coffee tables in cherry red lacquer. *Bottom left* The third group is a smaller, more intimate arrangement around the fireplace—two curved-back armchairs in natural leather and sofas in soft velvet. The paintings are by Gauguin and Modigliani.

House in Fort Worth, Texas. The informal family room looks out at the swimming pool on one side and a walled garden on the other. There are complete kitchen facilities behind the coromandel screen. The sectional seating, covered in off-white linen velvet, can be grouped in different ways.

A house in Bedford Hills, New York, designed by Edward L. Barnes. *Top* I don't usually like to arrange the seating in a living room around a fireplace, but it seemed the best solution in this case. *Bottom* I much prefer the less symmetrical arrangement I designed for the study in the same house. In addition to a big desk and a sofa seating group, I included a comfortable day bed for reading and naps. A wall of bookshelves with fabric-backed openings in which to display small figures and Mexican jewelry ties the whole arrangement together.

A house in Southampton, New York. I designed this house as well as the interiors, so we were able to plan ahead for seating and create two separate groups, accommodating gatherings of two or twelve. A single fiber rug ties the whole thing together, as does the use of some of the same chairs and fabrics in both groups. The pivoting armchairs are from the collection of my furniture produced by Jack Lenor Larsen.

Right A co-op in Sarasota, Florida. A long wall of books ties together the two seating groups which features furniture I designed for the collection produced by Jack Lenor Larsen. In the foreground is a pair of pivoting "Bub" chairs upholstered in off-white textured fabric; near the window are two Warwick cane-back lounge chairs.

Left An old, extensively remodeled Spanish-style house in Coconut Grove, Florida. A comfortable conversation group at the one end of the original screened loggia includes a circle of Bielecky willow armchairs with small wire tables for drinks; at the other end, which is used for dining, I added barbecue facilities. The floor is the original Cuban tile from the old house. I designed the wall light fixtures to provide a warm overall light at night.

133

Architectural Built-ins

I have always tried to build into the architecture as much storage
as possible—for books, hi-fi equipment, supplies, clothes, linen, and
kitchen needs—to avoid the need for freestanding pieces of furniture
and free the spaces of clutter.

A Chicago co-op owned by a pianist.
Sheet music is housed in this custom-
designed cabinet built flush with the
face of the fireplace. Shallow shelves
in sliding grooves pull out for easy
access. The end unit contains a small
bar behind the drop-front. On the
lower shelf is part of the owner's large
collection of American Indian baskets.
Also displayed are primitive and
modern works of art, including paintings by Picasso and Paul Klee.

My apartment on Central Park West in New York. *Top* In the guest room I constructed niches flush with an existing beam to create a shelf for writing and a storage section with shelves. Half of this I used for books and display of paintings and the other half for clothes. A sliding door provided access to the latter. Subway grating hides the built-in radiator. The painting is by Hans Hofmann. *Bottom* The view from my bedroom into the living room. When opened away from the living area, the floor-to-ceiling pivoting panel door folds back to cover the linen closet; when used to close off the bedroom, it exposes a white Temlite blind that covers the storage area. The niche at the end of this storage wall has glass and felt-covered shelves for the display of art objects; behind the shelves is an African textile.

Tandy Corporation offices, Fort Worth, Texas. Mr. Tandy's private lounge is fitted out with a sleepable sofa for naps and a big floppy Italian chair in natural leather for cigar-smoking. In the spaces created by columns, I built in shelves with recessed lighting for display.

A New York townhouse. The dining room doubles as a library—a combination I have always liked. Low storage cabinets were built flush with the walls and the shelves above set back so the books would be washed with incandescent light, giving a warm glow to the room.

A south side Chicago house. A b
in shelf at one end of the dining room
can be used for display, as shown here,
or to provide extra serving space.

A New York townhouse. In the master
bedroom a freestanding storage unit
was designed to create a dressing area
between the sleeping area and the
bath. Books and a lighted niche face
the bedroom, while drawers and cupboards with doors provide clothes
storage on the other side.

...ty of Architectural Detailing

...m a registered architect and have designed some houses and ...ther buildings from scratch, though most of my work has been re-designing existing structures and working as interior designer with other architects, including Harry Weese, Louis Kahn, and Edward L. Barnes. I have also designed a lot of furniture—custom-made items for clients as well as the Ben Baldwin Collection for Jack Lenor Larsen—and a series of gardens which is what I love most. In everything I do I strive for simplicity, both in concept and in detailing.

A shop for women's clothes in Montgomery, Alabama. The original building on the site had burned and had to be removed entirely. I designed a new facade in beige brick with display windows across the entire front, protected by a black-and-white striped awning.

A musician's house near Chicago. In the original design a balcony over the fireplace wall gave access to the bedrooms. I extended this balcony around the entire room, providing a place for guests to sit during musical recitals and giving scale to the high-ceilinged space. Shelves for books and sheet music run from floor to ceiling on the end wall. The simple railing repeats the rhythm of the roof joists.

A Miami bank. The wood-paneled stair and end-of-a-hall niche for displaying art are typical of the simple detailing I have used in my jobs.

A house in Southampton, New York.
Left The smoke blue color of this
house's stucco exterior is an integral
part of my design. Double doors open
from the living and dining rooms
onto a large terrace with a trellis for
white wisteria. *Above* The front entrance with its flush door set between
symmetrical panels of glass is typical
of the simple details used throughout
the house.

A house in Sarasota, Florida. I designed an addition to this house as well as the interiors, the furnishings, and the garden. *Left* The exterior of the house as seen from a trellised enclosure at poolside. *Below left* The front entrance. *Below right* A large, glass-enclosed room adjacent to the terrace contains a reflecting pool.

Below View of the garden. *Right* Two seating groups in the dining room. *Bottom right* In the dining room built-in shelf provides a space to display art objects.

Other Typical Features

Other typical features of my design work include minimal use of patterned fabrics, the predominance of quiet neutral colors, and flowing spaces.

A lady's dressing room. I introduced a yellow and natural Fortuny pattern on and behind the dressing table to add some color and curves.

A house in Coconut Grove, Florida. The neutral colors in the master bedroom are typical of my work. Natural linen, cotton, leather, and natural wood are my favorite materials. In this long room I built a freestanding headboard with a niche on the bed side and clothes storage behind in the passage leading to the bathroom. The original cypress doors and baseboards were kept and refinished in natural tones.

My house on North State Street in Chicago. In response to a magazine's request for a blue and white scheme, I used a Matisse-like print with white leaves on a blue ground on the sofa, two cushions, and the window panels in the living-dining room.

A house in Coconut Grove, Florida. *Left* A partition which is open at the top divides the living and dining areas. The balcony serves to humanize the scale of the high wood-beamed ceiling. *Above* Open passages on either side of the partition allow for the free flow of light and movement between the two areas.

An apartment in New York. *Above* A neutral color scheme enhances the feeling of openness while the area of dropped ceiling around the perimeter of the room helps focus attention on the owner's art collection. *Right* Instead of a solid wall, freestanding bookcases with clean, simple lines divide the dining area from the hall.

The executive offices of the Tandy
Corporation, Fort Worth, Texas. Here
the walls were either travertine or
white oak paneling and so beautiful
in themselves that there seemed to
be no need for art on the walls. The
light-colored wool carpeting, natural
wood tables, black leather chairs,
and terra-cotta clay pots for the trees
create a harmonious neutral scheme.

Antiques with Modern

For me furniture is either beautiful or ugly, comfortable or uncomfortable, and this has nothing to do with when it was made. In designing my collection for Jack Lenor Larsen, I tried to produce designs of classic simplicity which are comfortable, have sculptural interest, and look at home in any kind of interior.

A house in Minnesota designed by Edward L. Barnes. The four-poster bed, bergère chairs, and Spanish sofa mix beautifully with the glass-top metal table and complement the house's ultimate simplicity.

A grand house in Fort Worth, Texas, designed by I. M. Pei. *Left* I used the owners' set of baroque dining chairs with a custom-made table with burl elm top and steel bases. In the foreground is an informal dining area. *Below* In the master bedroom I used my Vicenza armchairs painted green-blue with an antique Italian desk. The yellow cabinet of drawers, under the Georgia O'Keeffe painting, was custom made.

Right A New York apartment. Old and new live in complete harmony.

Art in Interiors

Since I have always been keenly interested in painting and sculpture, I try to use works of art in my jobs—even if only good lithographs or prints.

Boardroom in the New York Philharmonic building at Lincoln Center in New York. The large painting is by Okada. The carpet was custom designed and made by V'soske, and the curtains are a Fortuny print in yellow and natural.

A house in Wayzata, Minnesota. Small sculptures in bronze and an Italian library ladder, which is a work of art in itself, grace the living area.

A house I designed in Southampton, New York. In the hallway is a Picasso print in a symmetrical arrangement with a bronze horse and bull and a mixed bouquet.

Bank offices in Miami, Florida. In the dining room (shared with Katcher law offices) a subdued color scheme goes well with a beautiful lithograph by Jim Dine.

A New York apartment. A portrait by William Beechey is a strong point of interest in the living room. In front of the portrait is a seating group of five of my pivoting upholstered armchairs.

151

Kitchens

As more and more people have to manage with less help, kitchens have become an integral part of living. I have designed kitchens ranging from elaborate centers for experiment and demonstration to tiny spaces in city apartments with hardly more than a stove, sink, and small refrigerator. I have always insisted that these spaces be up to the design standards of the rest of the house or apartment and be cheerful places to spend time.

My apartment on Central Park West in New York. I designed floor-to-ceiling storage with shallow shelves for glassware, dishes, liquor, and food supplies. A small table with comfortable chairs provides a spot for having breakfast and lunch.

A house in Coconut Grove, Florida. I opened up the space behind a circular stair so that the kitchen opens directly into the breakfast area. Bar stools provide seating at the freestanding work counter. For the floor I kept the original ceramic tiles from Cuba.

The cooking wing on Craig Claiborne's house in East Hampton, New York. Everything here is geared to professional cooking, experimentation, and demonstration. A wok range was installed for Chinese cooking, and there is a special counter for electrical gadgets, each with its own outlet.

Furniture and Products

The Ben Baldwin Collection

I have always designed custom furniture for specific situations on my jobs, but in 1978 I was asked by Jack Lenor Larsen to do a Ben Baldwin Collection which would be manufactured, displayed, and distributed by his company. It was the company's first venture into furniture production.

Left Ben Baldwin Collection for Jack Lenor Larsen. *Below* Sitting in one of my chairs.

RITZ SEATING

I expanded the design concept of the chairs I had designed for The Bar at the Ritz Hotel in Boston to include armchairs and sidechairs, with low or high backs, either upholstered or caned, in a variety of finishes, including anodized colors. Later a bar stool and tables in a variety of heights were added.

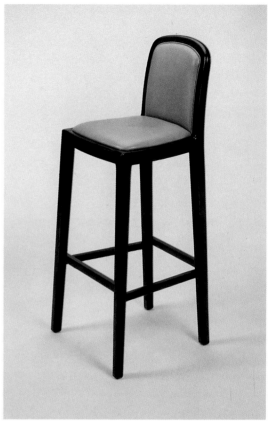

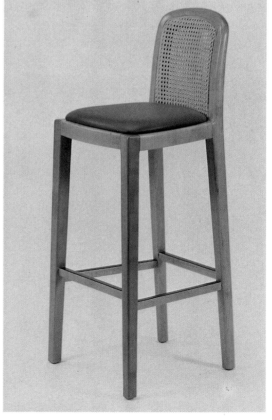

The Warwick group includes lounge chairs, dining-height armchairs, and a settee, all with cane or upholstered backs.

My upholstered lounge furniture (with plain or chanelled backs) includes a sofa in different sizes, an armchair, an ottoman, and a lounge chair that is also available in a smaller-scale version called the Bub chair (Baldwin Tub).

This group includes a slim-arm sofa and settee with a matching lounge chair.

This group of tables has metal bases with a band of openwork just beneath the top surface, which is available in a variety of materials. The museum seating group was designed in components for maximum flexibility (drawing by Ben Baldwin, 1991).

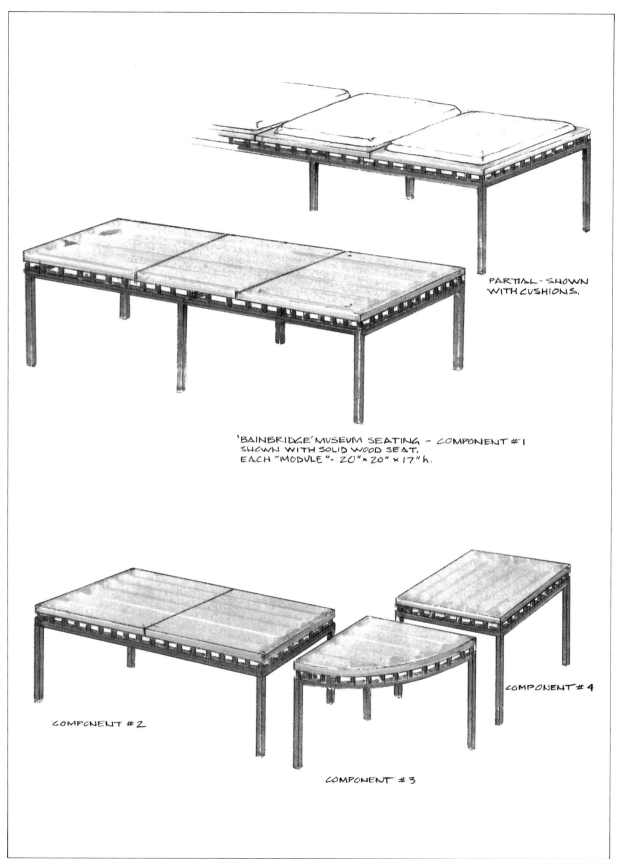

PARTIAL - SHOWN WITH CUSHIONS.

'BAINBRIDGE' MUSEUM SEATING - COMPONENT #1
SHOWN WITH SOLID WOOD SEAT.
EACH "MODULE"- 20"× 20"× 17"h.

COMPONENT #2

COMPONENT #3

COMPONENT #4

COMO TABLE

This round travertine table had a
pedestal base.

Product Designs

My product designs emphasize abstract flower and plant forms and include fabrics, china, candleholders, vases, and tables.

This page, top Design for a tablecloth; *center* Metal candleholders, table base, and vases; *bottom* Plant pan. *Opposite page, top* Three-legged lamp, folding tables/benches; *center* Cocktail table, slat table; *bottom* Folding stool, designs for dessert plates.

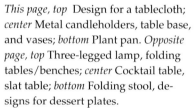

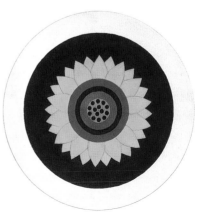

Rooms Without Roofs

Rooms Without Roofs

Gardening is a very important part of my life. I want the place where I live to be a sanctuary of peace and calm. I want to keep my life and my work close to nature—simple and free from rules. In nature one can refresh one's heart and seek spiritual calm and tranquility. Nowhere can this need for solitude be better satisfied than in the seclusion of a quiet garden.

A garden is a highly personal place, providing the greatest of all freedoms: privacy. For me the ultimate expression of privacy in nature is the roof terrace of Luis Barragán's house in Mexico. High, plain walls free of any symbolic decoration surround a garden with only the changing sky overhead. I know of no designer whose work so strongly affirms man's connection with nature—with earth, sky, water, and plants. This poetic man and his work are a continual inspiration to me.

It is sad indeed that privacy is so poorly thought of in this country that the building of high walls on property lines is forbidden, and, instead of having outdoor extensions of our indoor living spaces, we have to settle for the endless bare and exposed front yards of suburbia with its miles of foundation plantings.

In a garden one can experience both architecture and the universal aspects of nature. The art of landscape as we know it today is strongly architectural; a designer of gardens is usually given the title of landscape architect. In my own gardens, I have emphasized the contrasts between the natural elements of the landscape (earth, water, and plants) and fabricated architectural elements. The latter act as fixed and permanent concentration points in the garden's world of changing shapes, colors, sounds, and smells. The architectural elements do not compete with nature but make its impact stronger.

We can learn much from the gardens of other cultures—the gardens of Japan, so beautifully related to the adjoining architecture; the ancient gardens of China, designed by philosophers and poets, in which each element had symbolic significance (many of the plants in my gardens were favorites in Chinese gardens: iris, daylilies, hibiscus, poppies, peonies, lotus, lilies, hosta, bamboo, ginkgo and pine trees); the quiet, peaceful wall-enclosed gardens of Central and South America and of the countries around the Mediterranean.

If I had to state my feeling about garden design briefly, I would say that there should be variety in the layout and simplicity in the planting. There should be a number of different places to see and visit, and there should be unexpected surprises. But the simpler the plant-ing—large areas of one or a few plants—the better. In my own gardens I have used large areas of lace-cap hydrangea, rhododendron, iris, pachysandra, and hosta to provide both color and texture, and thus enrich the design. Lastly, empty space is as important outside as it is inside, and just as luxurious; it signifies peaceful silence.

I have been involved in many aspects of design during my lifetime—painting, sculpture, architecture, interiors, furniture, fabrics, stage sets, landscape, and gardens. In the end I have come to feel that landscape design and gardens are the ultimate form of creativity. The vocabulary is universal and so is the audience, almost everyone enjoys looking at a beautiful garden. Even the names of the plants, like *Thunbergia grandiflora alba* or *Campanula persicifolia,* are beautiful.

With a bit of effort anyone can learn the basic fundamentals of gardening. The facts about climate, orientation, soil, sunlight, insects, food, and water are available from books or can be learned simply by looking and doing. But creating a beautiful garden or landscape requires sensibilities of the highest order and a personal involvement with nature and its elements.

I believe that training in architecture is the best foundation for a landscape designer. He or she must deal with the same basic principles an architect considers—the site, the requirements of the client, orientation, changing patterns of light, color and texture, scale, the use of sculpture and other decorative objects, the detailing of architectural elements such as gazebos, arbors, and trellises. In gardens one has the bonus of the sound of birds and water, the ever-changing shadows, the sky and reflections of it in water, as well as the added challenge of changes in the structure of a garden from one season to the next. A garden is never static but is in a constant state of change. Flowers bloom and fade, the seasons bring waves of different colors and textures. A good garden must be beautiful in winter, when many branches are bare and its skeletal form takes over, and in summer, when the rich fullness of shapes and colors predominates.

Garden design also has a lot in common with designing interiors. One deals with plants instead of furniture but in both cases with spaces and with the relationship of different spaces to each other, with solids and voids, with volumes, masses, textures, and colors. My gardens have a great deal of green, with accents of color. So I try to vary the shades of green and the shapes and textures of the leaves.

It would be impossible for me to explain how to design a garden. One just feels when it is right. Everything has to work together, and

Huntting Lane, East Hampton

Above Overall view showing long arbor at upper level. *Facing page, top* Views of sunken garden in ruins of old basement. Wide stairs connected two levels of redwood decks. *Bottom* View from the sunken garden toward the house.

one knows when it does. However, I have found the following to be useful guidelines:

- work with plant material that will be happy growing wherever the garden is. My garden in Long Island is very different from the one in Florida because there is a different choice of plants with which to work. In Florida there are usually one or two nights of freezing weather in the winter, and this can destroy the whole garden overnight. I have had to start from scratch several times in Florida, but there are also destructive hurricanes on Long Island. So one has to do a lot of experimenting to find plants one likes that will survive nature's periodic lapses of cooperation.
- reduce maintenance by using a lot of paving. This is practical and makes walking, working, and hauling things around easier. It also gives architectural scale to the garden.
- be ruthless. First of all, learn to say "no" to people who want to give you things you don't want, and if you find that some plant you've put in isn't right, snatch it out.
- realize that a garden will, and should, change. Move things around when you see that they would look better another way. A garden is never "finished."

Gardens may, indeed, never be finished. But I can't complain. They're what I love most.

Facing page, clockwise from top left My sculpture *Homage to Luis Barragán* overlooks reflecting pool with a jet of water. Under the arbor. The reflecting pool. Path to sundial surrounded by roses. *Above* Looking toward the arbor past Corten steel sculpture by Marcia Weese.

Above The arbor at the front of the house. *Right* Another view of the front arbor, which ended in a screened gazebo; pale yellow Hyperion daylilies fill the planting bed.

Facing page, top Single hollyhocks around the sundial; *bottom* In the wild garden a rope hammock hangs in the shade of sycamore trees. *Below* Oakleaf hydrangea planted beneath the old arbor.

Facing page A walled courtyard off the guest room. The double seat was inspired by Persian miniatures; Phoenix palm in a bed of aspidistra and giant bamboo behind the wall. *Above and left* South facade, facing the lagoon. Custom lattice adds to the tropical feeling and acts as a railing for the balcony of the upstairs workroom.

Outside the entrance a large Italian pottery jar nestles in the planting of penta and rosemary with bamboo in the background. The sharp geometry of the ceramic floor tile contrasts with the looseness of the planting outside.

Facing page, clockwise from top left Aspidistra and liriope surround one of the concrete water basins. Platform at the edge of the lagoon; cypress planters at the four corners hold silver-grey Texas sage. A friendly grey heron stands watch, hoping for a fish. *Above and top right* The arbor off the living room; the vine with flowers hanging down in long racemes is beautiful blue *Thunbergia grandiflora. Bottom right* Walled garden with the "Persian" gazebo; large clay pots hold calamondin oranges and bananas.

185

McGillicuddy Garden, Sarasota

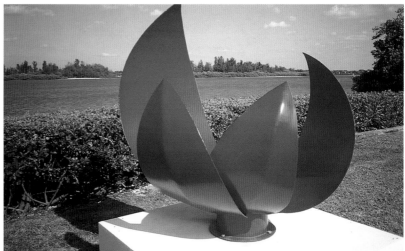

Clockwise from top left Mexican flamevine grows on a trellis at the edge of a bed of penta and roses. Swimming pool overlooking the bay with arbors on both sides. View from the covered space beneath the upstairs master bedroom. Flower form sculpture I designed for the garden.

Maynard Garden, Southampton

Above Rose garden with reflecting pool and lotus fountain by Marcia Weese.
Left Looking east from the terrace at the rose garden.

Palma Terrace, East Hampton

Left The gate to the front entrance.
Above The front entrance, surrounded by lattice enclosing wooden seats on either side; brick terraces on two levels.

Clockwise from top left The side garden off the kitchen has a bronze flower sculpture by Marcia Weese nestled in plantings of rhododendron and oakleaf hydrangea; *Clematis spooneri* on the fence behind. New Dawn roses on the arches behind the central area. Looking under the big crabapple tree to the front garden. The deck overlooking the back garden; *Clematis maximowicziana* blooming on the arches in September.

Clockwise from top left The deck with pink *Clematis montana* in bloom. Arches covered with white morning glories and moonflowers. One of the sculptures in the garden.

Purple sage and Japanese iris in the
herb garden.

Afterword

A courtly and sophisticated yet simple and meditative man, Ben once said that "Design is my means of expressing what I believe. It is my means of contributing whatever I have to contribute toward making the world a better place to live." His work is not easily categorized. It displays neither a readily recognizable style nor a single design approach but is instead a subtle synthesis of classic design principles and originality. An architect by training, Ben believed interior design to be an architectural process in which the first concern is with space and the challenge is to create a poetic arrangement of solids and voids, color and texture, light and dark that will delight the senses. A gardener by avocation, he also believed that the ideal house was a simple shelter in a garden—an uncluttered refuge from the chaos and confusion of the world, in which one could work and think and relax and be creative. It was his hope that this book would be a record of his constant striving to achieve that ideal.

Kitty Baldwin W eese

Chronology of the Life of Benjamin Baldwin

1913   Born, Montgomery, Alabama, on March 29

1925-28   Starke's University School, Montgomery
Traveled in U.S.A. and Canada with grandparents

1928-31   Lawrenceville Preparatory School, Lawrenceville, New Jersey
Staff writer for The LIT
Pipe and Quill Literary Club
Bibliophiles (Library Group)
Choir
Periwig Dramatic Club

Trips to Bermuda (spring breaks)

First trip to Europe (summer 1930)

1931-35   Princeton University, Department of Architecture
Drawing and painting under Peter Teigen
Drama and movie critic for *Daily Princetonian*
Designed sets for Theatre Intime

Traveled in Germany and France with Avery Dulles (summer 1934)

A.B. degree in Architecture (1935)

1935-36   Studied painting under Hans Hofmann, New York City and Provincetown, Massachusetts

1936-38   Graduate school, Princeton University
Worked in architecture under Jean Labatut; drawing and painting under James E. Davis
Fontainebleau Scholarship (summer 1937)
Worked in sculpture under M. Gélin; worked with Jean Labatut on designs for fountains and fireworks for 1939 New York World's Fair; traveled in France
Junior Fellow in Architecture (1937-38)
A.I.A. Award for General Excellence in Architecture (1938)
Princeton Scholarship to Cranbrook Academy of Art
M.F.A. degree with Honors in Architecture (1938)
Thesis on housing in Montgomery, Alabama

1938-39   Cranbrook Academy of Art, Bloomfield Hills, Michigan
Worked under Eliel Saarinen in architecture and town planning; worked under Walter Curt Behrendt on studies for replanning waterfront in Buffalo, New York; worked in photography, ceramics, textiles, metal, and painting

1939-40   Office of Eliel and Eero Saarinen, Bloomfield Hills, Michigan
In charge of model for Smithsonian Art Gallery project

Exhibited textiles at New York World's Fair

Designed samples for Alabama's W.P.A. weaving project

Exhibited paintings at Princeton University and at Museum of Fine Arts, Montgomery, Alabama

Trip by car to West Coast with Wallace Mitchell and Marianne Strengell

1940-41   Private practice in architecture with Harry Weese in Kenilworth, near Chicago

Lived and had office in room attached to house of architect George Maher

Worked as designer and contractor doing small houses

Won First Place (furniture for outdoor living) and two Honorable Mentions (living-room furniture other than seating and furniture for a bedroom) in the Museum of Modern Art's competition for contemporary furnishings, "Organic Design"; jury included Edward Stone, Marcel Breuer, Catherine Bauer Wurster, Edgar Kaufmann, Jr., Frank Parrish, Alfred H. Barr, and Eliot Noyes

1941-45   Commissioned as ensign in U.S. Navy to work in Photo Interpretation (February 1942)

Naval Training School at Harvard University

Photo Interpretation School at Anacostia, Washington, D.C.

Fleet Air Wing N.A.S., Norfolk, Virginia

Fleet Air Wing, North Africa (French Morocco) (December 1942-October 1943)

Served as publications officer (articles, exhibitions, etc.), Photo Interpretation Center, Department of the Navy, Washington, D.C.

Lived in an apartment at 1703 21st Street, N.W.

1945-47   Worked as designer for Skidmore, Owings and Merrill, New York, on interiors, furniture, and complete furnishings for the Terrace Plaza Hotel, Cincinnati (1946)

Editorial representative and New York correspondent for the magazine *Arts and Ar chitectur e*, published in Los Angeles

Left Skidmore, Owings and Merrill (spring 1947)

1948-50 Set up independent design office-workshop in New York under the name Design Unit New York at 33 East 75th Street

Designed houses, interiors, furniture, and products

Formed association with William Machado and produced line of printed fabrics (distributed by Arundell Clarke), which were exhibited in the first "Good Design" show, designed by Charles Eames, at the Chicago Merchandise Mart

Weese-Baldwin tea cart shown in the exhibition "Modern Art in Your Life" at the Museum of Modern Art in New York (1949)

1951-54 Moved design office (Baldwin-Machado) to Montgomery, Alabama

Remodeled house at 622 Adams Street for living quarters and office

Specialized in architecture and interior design

Opened retail shop for contemporary furniture and furnishings on Perry Street in downtown Montgomery in connection with design office

Traveled in Europe; spent considerable time in Venice (summer 1952)

1955-63 Moved design office to Chicago

Lived in an apartment at 148 East Ontario Street

Worked first out of retail shop Baldwin Kingrey, operated by sister Kitty Weese and Jody Kingrey

Later shared office space with Richard Barringer on Erie Street

Designed interiors, display rooms, products, etc.

Traveled in Tangier, Portugal, Spain, Venice (summer 1956); to London (March 1957; S.S. United States); Spain, Greek Islands, Italy, especially the gardens around Florence, with William Machado (summer 1960), and with Ward Bennett (summer 1961)

1963-73 Moved to New York (July 1963)

Interior design and collaboration with architects on interiors

Completed house-studio for self in East Hampton, Long Island (July 1967)

Traveled in Europe with David Scholes (summer 1964; S.S. France)

Traveled around the world with Ward Bennett (five months in 1969-70)

Three trips to St. Maarten (1968-69)

1973-79 Remodeled house-studio for self in Sarasota

Resident half the year in East Hampton and half the year in Sarasota

Traveled with Jonathan Warwick in Hawaii doing research on gardens and plants (fall 1978)

Began writing a book about design work

Designed Ben Baldwin Collection of furniture for Jack Lenor Larsen, Inc., New York

Armchair, originally designed for Ritz Bar in Boston, won top award (1979)

Exhibition "Homage to Ben Baldwin" opened at Larsen showroom in New York, November 21, 1978

1981–91 Traveled in Italy (Milan Furniture Show), France, and Switzerland with Jonathan Warwick (fall 1981)

Ritz armchair included in exhibition devoted to Jack Lenor Larsen at the Musée des Arts Décoratifs, Musée du Louvre, Paris (October 1981)

Traveled to Los Angeles, San Diego, and San Francisco (1982)

Purchased property in Lido Shores, Sarasota, for which Luis Barragán and Raul Ferrera designed house (never built)

Work included in the exhibition "Design in America: The Cranbrook Vision, 1925-1950" at the Metropolitan Museum of Art in New York (1984)

Traveled to France, Italy, Germany, Yugoslavia, and London with Jonathan Warwick (September 1984)

Traveled to England to visit gardens with Richard Frederick (May 1984)

Designated Charter Member of *Interior Design* magazine's Hall of Fame for Interior Designers (December 1985); other charter members were Davis Allen, Florence Knoll Bassett, Mario Buatta, Barbary D'Arcy, Henry End, Arthur Gensler, Richard Himmel, Melanie Kahane, Lawrence Lerner, Mrs. Henry Parish II, Warren Platner, John Saladino, Michael Taylor, and Kenneth Walker

Traveled to Scandinavia, Leningrad, Vienna, Venice, and London with Jonathan Warwick (August-September 1987)

Traveled to the Caribbean (Antigua, Grenada, Barbados) with Tim Ivko (January 1991)

1993 Died, Sarasota, Florida, on April 4

Design Work

1940s

Remodeled top floor of house at 33 East 75th St., New York, for use as residence and office (Dorothy Noyes' shop New Design on ground floor)

Designed line of printed fabrics with William Machado (produced and distributed by Arundell Clarke)

Remodeled house-office for Baldwin-Machado in Montgomery, Alabama

1950s

Architecture and interiors for Danziger Department Store, Montgomery, Alabama

House for Mrs. J.M. Baldwin, Montgomery

House for Mrs. Walter Lobman, Montgomery

Baldwin-Machado shop, Montgomery

Interiors of house for Julian McGowin, Chapman, Alabama

Office for Julian McGowin, Chapman

Interiors of house for Pascal Shook, Birmingham, Alabama

Three model houses for Pascal Shook's development, Birmingham

Lakeside house for Dr. and Mrs. Robert Pye, Lake Jordan, Alabama

Apartment for Claire and Ernest Zeisler, Drake Tower, Chicago

Offices for Union Starch, Columbus, Indiana

Offices for Cummins Engine Company, Columbus, Indiana

Interiors of house for Clarence Hamilton, Columbus, Indiana

London office for Cummins Engine Company

Offices for Solo Cup Company, Chicago, New York, and Richmond, Virginia

Showroom for Hamilton (Cosco) Manufacturing Company, Furniture Mart, Chicago

Offices for Hamilton (Cosco), Columbus, Indiana

Interiors of house for George Newlin, Columbus, Indiana (Harry Weese, architect)

Interiors of house for Robert Hulseman, Winnetka, Illinois

Private plane for Solo Cup Company

Shop for Italian Court Flowers, Chicago

Sets for Chicago Opera "Galavante '59"

Apartment for Lewis Manilow, Chicago (not executed)

Interiors of house for Sage and John Cowles, Wayzata, Minnesota (Edward L. Barnes, architect)

Interiors of house for J. W. Getzels, Chicago

Remodeled house for Dr. and Mrs. Robert Pye, Woodland, California

Interiors of house for Mrs. Leo Roberg, Chicago

Remodeled house for self at 1243 North State Street, Chicago

1960s

Remodeled own apartment at 75 Central Park West, New York (published in *New York Times, Elle, Domus*)

Apartment for Mr. and Mrs. Charles Murphy, Jr., Lake Shore Drive, Chicago (C. F. Murphy Associates, architects)

Lobby of apartment building at 75 Central Park West

Apartment for Joan Kaplan Davidson, New York (not completed)

Apartment for Midu Brock, New York

Boardroom, Green Room, and Leonard Bernstein's dressing room for New York Philharmonic (served on design committee with Mrs. David Rockefeller and Mrs. Sterling Bunnell)

House for self in St. Maarten (not executed)

Office of the President at Yale University (not executed)

Presidents' Room at Yale

Apartment for Mr. and Mrs. Stanley Getzler, New York

Interiors of house for Mr. and Mrs. Leonard Garment, Brooklyn Heights, New York (Joseph Mertz, architect)

Apartment for Richard Skudstad, New York

The Bar at the Ritz Hotel, Boston

Studio-apartment for Adolph Gottlieb, New York

Interiors of house for Mr. and Mrs. Karl Kaysen (President of Institute for Advanced Studies, Princeton, New Jersey)

House-studio for self in East Hampton, New York (published in *New York Times, Architectural Digest, House and Garden, Elle, Domus,* and *Interior Design.* Moved in July 1967)

Remodeled studio-apartment for self at 425 East 51st Street, New York (Fall of 1967)

Interiors of house for Anne and Charles Tandy, Fort Worth, Texas (I. M. Pei, architect)

Furnishings for library and dining hall, Phillips Exeter Academy, Exeter, New Hampshire (Louis Kahn, architect)

Interiors of house for Mr. and Mrs. Volney Righter, Bedford Hills, New York (Edward L. Barnes, architect)

Interiors of townhouse with photo studio for Richard Avedon, New York

Showroom for Lacour-Denno, New York

Interiors for Walter Thayer House (Edward L. Barnes, architect; not executed)

1970s

Remodeled house-studio for self in Sarasota, Florida (published in *Architectural Digest* and *House and Garden*)

Remodeling and interiors of house for Gerald Katcher, Coconut Grove, Florida (published in *Interiors*)

Interiors for Yale Center for British Art, New Haven, Connecticut (Louis Kahn, architect)

Remodeling and interiors of First National Bank of Greater Miami

Top floor of executive offices for Tandy Corporation, Fort Worth, Texas

Remodeled house for Mr. and Mrs. Dennis McGillicuddy, Sarasota, Florida

Furnishings of apartment for Albert Fuller, New York

Remodeling and furnishings of apartment for Gregory Smith, New York

Furnishings of house for Mr. and Mrs. Stephen DuBrul, New York (with Jonathan Warwick)

Ben Baldwin Furniture Collection for Jack Lenor Larsen, New York

Three-story cooking wing of house for Craig Claiborne, East Hampton, New York

Remodeling and interiors of United National Bank of Miami

Architecture, interiors, and garden of house for Mrs. Walter Maynard, Southampton, New York (published in *House and Garden*)

Interiors and furnishings for Americana Hotel, Fort Worth (with Roger Ferri and Jonathan Warwick)

Interiors and furnishings for Museum of Fine Arts, Dallas (Edward L. Barnes, architect)

Interiors of Richardson Foundation, Fort Worth

1980s

Remodeled house for Gregory Smith in East Hampton, New York (with Jonathan Warwick)

Interiors for "Nine Hotel Project" for People's Republic of China (not executed)

Interiors and furnishings for law firm of Katcher, Scharlin and Lanzetta, Miami (with Jonathan Warwick)

Addition to house for Françoise and Soulima Stravinsky, Sarasota, Florida

Addition to house, interiors, furnishings, and landscape for Mr. and Mrs. Dennis McGillicuddy, Sarasota

Remodeling and furnishings of apartment for Mr. and Mrs. Ralph Stevens, Sarasota

Garden of house for Stephen Swid, Southampton, New York

House for self, Lido Shores, Florida (not executed)

Project for fifty retail shops worldwide for Calvin Klein (with Luis Barragán and Raul Ferrera; not executed)

Second remodeling of house-studio for self in Sarasota

Second house and garden for self in East Hampton

Bibliography

PERIODICALS (design work)

New York Times, magazine section, 4/24/49, 11/23/78, 9/17/50,
    4/11/65, 12/6/64

Architectural Record, 6/49, 6/77

Interiors, 8/50, 2/51, 3/75, 2/79

Ladies Home Journal, 11/51

Better Homes and Gardens, 11/51

House and Garden, 4/65, 6/70, 11/70, 4/74, 3/86

House Beautiful, 4/93

Fortune, 3/66

Elle, 3/66

Domus, 3/66, 5/70

Schöner Wohnen, 1/68

Architectural Digest, 3/76, 1/79, 11/79

Residential Interiors, 3/76

House and Garden Decoration Guide (Spring 1979)

Interior Design, 6/79, 1/79

House and Garden's Best in Decoration 1987

Oculus (A.I.A.) 45, no. 8

Also mentioned or illustrated in:

AIA Journal

Architectural Forum

Architectural Review

Arts & Architecture

Bauen & Wohnen

Chicago

Everyday Art Quarterly

Progressive Architecture

Vogue

BOOKS (design work)

Organic Design, exhibition catalogue (New York: Museum of Modern Art, 1940)

Nelson, George. *Living Spaces* (New York: Whitney Publications, 1952)

O'Brien, George. *New York Times Book of Interior Decoration* (New York: Farrar, Straus and Girous, 1965)

Plumb, Barbara. *Young Design in Living* (New York: Viking Press, 1969)

Smith, C. Ray. *Supermannerism: New Attitudes in Post-modern Architecture* (New York: Dutton, 1977)

Design in America : The Cranbrook Vision, 1925-1950, exhibition catalogue (New York: Abrams in association with the Detroit Institute of Arts and the Metropolitan Museum of Art, 1983)

Smith, C. Ray. *Interior Design in Twentieth Century America* (New York: Harper & Row, 1987)

Verey, Rosemary. *The American Man's Garden* (Boston: Little, Brown, 1990)

Encyclopedia of American Art

PERIODICALS (Baldwin-Machado fabrics)

Interiors, 4/49, 9/49, 1/50, 2/51, 6/50, 5/49

Everyday Art Quarterly, summer 1949

House and Garden, 9/49, 10/49, 3/50, 4/50

Retailing Daily, 9/6/49, 4/18/50

New York Herald Tribune, 12/28/49, 4/13/50, 5/25/52, 5/3/50, 5/25/52

Interior Design, 1/50

The New Yorker, 3/11/50

New York Times, 4/13/50, 4/9/50, 4/13/52, 2/12/50

Vogue, 4/15/50

Sunday News (New York), 4/16/50

Home Furnishings Merchandising, 5/50

House Beautiful, 6/50

Milwaukee Journal, 1950

Arts & Architecture, 12/51

Pageant, 9/52

EXHIBITIONS (Baldwin-Machado fabrics)

House designed by Marcel Breuer in the Museum of Modern Art's Garden, 1949

"Good Design," Merchandise Mart, Chicago, 1949

"For Modern Living," Detroit Institute of Arts, 1949

"Ceramics and Textiles," Scripps College, Claremont, California, 1950

"Inside—1950," Philadelphia Art Alliance, 1950

Haiti Bicentennial Exposition, Haiti, 1950

"3rd Biennial Exhibition of Textiles and Ceramics," Museum, Cranbrook Academy of Arts, 1951

"Industrie und Handwerk Schaffen," Stuttgart, Germany, 1951

"New Design Trends" Museum of Modern Art, New York, 1952

"Design for Use, USA," Grand Palais, Paris, 1952

"Under Every Roof," Denver Art Museum

"Modern Textiles," Walker Art Center, Minneapolis

"The Design Exhibition," Denver Art Museum

"Good Design in Industry," Institute of Contemporary Arts, Boston

"New Design Trends," Museum of Modern Art, New York

Institute of Contemporary Arts, Washington, D.C.

Columbus Gallery of Fine Arts, Columbus, Ohio

Photo Credits